What's it like to work in the biggest hit in years? In this delightful book based on his almost daily notes, Jeffry Denman tells the story of a year in one performer's life, from his job in the final days of *Cats* (now and forever, but finally closed) to a small but promising part in the Mel Brooks smash. Nathan Lane and Matthew Broderick, Mel Brooks and Anne Bancroft, Susan Stroman, Gary Beach, and Roger Bart are all here in Jeffry Denman's story. We follow *The Producers* — from its first casting call to the Chicago tryouts, we watch as numbers are cut and roles reassigned; we are there at the record-breaking New York opening, and then at the Tony awards (where the show won in more categories than any show in Tony history).

What makes this book special is that we watch through Jeffry Denman's eyes — not from the star's perspective but the view from the chorus. Denman takes on several small roles in the show: the Blind Violinist; the Little Wooden Boy; FDR; a little old lady dancing with a walker; and Scott, the choreographer. We get to see director Susan Stroman coaching and Mel Brooks laughing (or not) at Denman's comic turns. What works? What doesn't? How does all that energy and talent translate into the show you still can't get tickets for?

A Year with The Producers takes us up to Jeffry Denman's big break, when he goes on for Matthew Broderick in the role of Leo Bloom, the nerdy accountant who dreams of being a producer. It's a moment every young actor will read with terror and delight.

A behind-the-scenes story with more than a touch of theatrical magic about it, *A Year with The Producers* is a book for actors and theater fans everywhere.

A Year With

The

PRODUCERS

ONE ACTOR'S EXHAUSTING
(BUT WORTH IT) JOURNEY
FROM *CATS* TO
MEL BROOKS'
MEGA-HIT

By **Jeffry Denman**

FOREWORD BY
MATTHEW BRODERICK

A Theatre Arts Book
ROUTLEDGE
New York and London

A Theatre Arts Book

Published in 2002 by
Routledge
29 West 35th Street
New York, NY 10001

Published in Great Britain by
Routledge
11 New Fetter Lane
London EC4P 4EE

Routledge is an imprint of the Taylor & Francis Group.

Printed on acid-free, 250-year-life paper.
Manufactured in the United States of America.

10 9 8 7 6 5 4 3 2

Library of Congress Cataloging-in-Publication Data is available from the Library
of Congress.

A Year with The Producers / Jeffry Denman
ISBN 0-878-30154-2

Photographs on pages 55, 65, 80, 84, 86, 93, 94, 132, 137, 158 by Paul Kolnik;
page 155 by Jeffry Denman; page 170 by Ashley Horne; pages 18, 23, 24
by Bob Denman; pages 75, 76, 141 by Matt Loehr; page 187 by
Kristin Hoebermann; back cover photograph by Melissa Rae Mahon.

When I began writing this book it was easy for me to decide who to dedicate it to: my cousin, Patty Denman-Krahling, whose life and spirit live on in the hearts of every member of my family.

However, I wrote my last journal entry on September 10, 2001. The next day, we all woke up to an event that forever changed the lives, spirits, and hearts of the country, and of most of the world. As Arthur Miller wrote, "Attention must be paid."

And so I dedicate this book to the memory of the people we've lost, my one and our many, and to the lives of the people who had to go on without them.

CONTENTS

FOREWORD

When you're in a show like *The Producers*, you're a part of something so full of energy that it isn't always easy to take a step back and see how you — and it — got there. Jeff Denman had the good idea of keeping a journal — something many of us wish we had done and hardly ever take the time to do.

Jeff and I worked together in my first Broadway musical, *How to Succeed in Business Without Really Trying*. I didn't see a lot of him, though, because he was an offstage understudy, what we call a swing. Now we're on the same stage in *The Producers*. I play Leo Bloom opposite Nathan Lane's Max Bialystock. And Jeff? Jeff plays a blind violinist, a terrible choreographer, a little old lady in a walker, FDR, a guy auditioning to play the Führer in "Springtime for Hitler," and a Nazi or two. Not a lot of lines, but a lot of work.

I've never been in the ensemble of a Broadway show. As Leo Bloom, I've got to have a big picture. But the ensemble is about having a lot of little pictures and making them all fit into the frame. Reading Jeff's account of how *The Producers* got put together I'm reminded of what is too easy to forget. I'm thinking, for example, of how tough it was to get that blanket drop right in the Leo-Ulla scene in act two (*note to Jeff*: the trick is in the way Leo puts the blanket into his pocket a few minutes earlier). So much effort goes into a routine we try to make the audience think is second nature. If you read what Jeff has to say about a few seconds on stage as FDR, you'll see what I mean. All big shows work this way. *The Producers* is no exception.

Jeff's year begins with *Cats*, a show he joined in its final Broadway life. It ends when he goes on one weekend for, er, me as Leo Bloom. He's proud of getting that blue blanket drop in all four performances. He should be.

Jeff doesn't say it's his favorite year, but he comes close. Anyone who has been in an ensemble or an audition will recognize Jeff's story. Anyone who has seen a Broadway show and wondered how it gets put together will enjoy the backstage view. Like everyone else in the theater, Jeff's love of performing gets him on stage. I think that comes through on the pages that follow. I hope you'll enjoy reading them. And see a Broadway show soon.

Matthew Broderick
December 2001

CAST OF CHARACTERS

The Cast of The Producers

Nathan Lane	Max Bialystock
Matthew Broderick	Leo Bloom
Gary Beach	Roger DeBris
Cady Huffman	Ulla
Ron Orbach/Brad Oscar	Franz Liebkind
Roger Bart	Carmen Ghia
Madeleine Doherty	Hold-Me Touch-Me
Kathy Fitzgerald	Shirley Markowitz, Jury Foreman, Kiss-Me Feel-Me
Eric Gunhus	Lead Tenor
Peter Marinos	Bryan, Jack Lepidus, Judge
Jennifer Smith	Usherette, Lick-Me Bite-Me
Ray Wills	Mr. Marks, Kevin, Jason Green, Gunther, *Max Bialystock* u/s
Jeffry Denman	Blind Violinist, Scott, Donald Dinsmore, Guard, *Leo Bloom* u/s, *Franz Liebkind* u/s
Bryn Dowling	Usherette
Robert Fowler	Unhappiest Accountant, O'Houlihan
Ida Leigh Curtis	Ensemble, *Ulla* u/s
Kimberly Hester	Ensemble
Naomi Kakuk	Ensemble
Matt Loehr	O'Riley
Angie Schworer	Ensemble, *Ulla* u/s
Abe Sylvia	Ticket Taker, O'Rourke, Bailiff
Tracy Terstriep	Ensemble

Swings/Understudies

Jim Borstelmann	Male swing, *Franz Liebkind* u/s, *Roger DeBris* u/s
Adrienne Gibbons	Female swing
Jamie LaVerdiere	Male swing, *Leo Bloom* u/s, *Carmen Ghia* u/s
Brad Musgrove	Dance Captain, Male swing, *Roger DeBris, Carmen Ghia* u/s
Christina Marie Norrup	Dance Captain, Female swing

Creative Personnel for The Producers

Mel Brooks	Composer/Lyricist and Author
Tom Meehan	Coauthor
Susan Stroman	Director/Choreographer
Robin Wagner	Set Design
William Ivey Long	Costume Design
Peter Kaczorowski	Lighting Design
Steve Kennedy	Sound Design
Steven Zweigbaum	Associate Director/Production Stage Manager
Ira Mont	Stage Manager
Casey Eileen Rafter	Assistant Stage Manager
Warren Carlyle	Associate Choreographer
Lisa Shriver	Assistant Choreographer
Paul Huntley	Wig and Hair Design
Glen Kelly	Musical Arrangements and Supervision
Patrick Brady	Music Direction and Vocal Arrangements
Doug Besterman	Orchestrations

The Producers of The Producers

Richard Frankel, Steven Baruch, Tom Viertel, Marc Routh, Bob and Harvey Weinstein, Rocco Landesman, Rick Steiner, Doug Meyer, James Stern, Robert Sillerman, and Fredric and Rhonda Mayerson

Supporting Cast and Topics

Bob and Maggie Denman	Parents
Bob and Gregg	Brothers
Anne and Vicky	Brothers' wives, respectively
Ann Steele	Agent
Dennis Stowe and Nancy Lemenager	Best friends
Brother Fred Dihlmann	Teacher, mentor, dear friend
OB	Stage Manager of *Cats*
Johnson-Liff Casting	Casting Associates (Geoffrey Johnson, Vinnie Liff, Tara Rubin) for *Cats* and *The Producers*
Dancing in the Dark	Musical I've written
Cats	Long-running show I'm in at the beginning of this book

I HAVE AN AUDITION

THE PHONE RINGS. I can't answer it. I'm in the midst of "Love Can't Happen" from *Grand Hotel*. It's opening night on Broadway and I'm playing the Count. Alright, alright, I'm in my living room, but it's still a damn good performance. Guilt gets the better of me; I turn off the CD player and pick up. It's Tara Rubin from Johnson-Liff Casting. She would like me to come in for *The Producers*. I say yes. It's the most talked-about show for the coming season. I've been keeping an eye on its development for a few years, being a huge fan of the film. If this were to go well, the timing would be perfect. *Cats* is coming to a close and I haven't really thought about what I'm going to do down the line. From what I know, Susan Stroman is directing and choreographing. Mel Brooks is writing the book, music, and lyrics. That surprises me. I didn't know Mel Brooks knew how to write music.

Susan Stroman is someone with whom I have had a kind of love-hate relationship ever since first discovering her work. I am sure this has more to do with my own insecurities than anything she actually does or does not feel toward me. I loved her work on *Crazy for You* and immediately admired her. Being familiar with Fred Astaire films, I see a lot of Astaire's influence in her work. I felt like I was a perfect candidate for one of her shows. When I first got to the city in 1994 I went to the open call for Hal Prince's *Show Boat*, which she choreographed. I did well. The final callback consisted of three African-American men and me. I figured either I had it in the bag or someone didn't look closely at my headshot. I didn't get it. Then in 1996 I auditioned for

Kander and Ebb's *Steel Pier*. This time I was at the invited audition — a step up from an open call. Susan separated us into couples and I learned a partnering combination. My partner and I didn't exactly click. Didn't get it. Hopefully, three's a charm.

When you are in a show that's closing, every new show you audition for acts as the best-case scenario. My friend Dennis Stowe says, "There's nothin' like signing your new contract in your current dressing room." You have a job and you've gotten another. So often actors will be out of work for weeks, months, even years before the next job comes around. I've been very lucky. I work hard and make sure that I am prepared and in the right place at the right time. That's half the battle right there, showing up. I've had auditions where I know I didn't do my best but got kept, others where I did do my best and got cut, and the far-too-infrequent times when you and the auditioners are on the same page: you do well and you get the job. But the last year and a half has been very good to me audition-wise. I've been on quite a roll. I'm confident that I will find something, *Producers* or otherwise.

So I get to audition again for "Stro." That's what people who have worked with Susan Stroman call her. People who haven't worked with her — but *want* to — call her "Stro" too. It sounds forced. I try to say "Susan Stroman" or at least "Stroman," — mainly because I don't know her. It seems to me you should earn the right to call her "Stro."

I am excited and apprehensive. Excited because of the opportunity. Apprehensive because I have been down this road before. During both the *Show Boat* and the *Steel Pier* auditions I felt as if she never saw me. I'm not suggesting she didn't physically see me standing or dancing there. It's more of an intuitive thing. You *know* when they are watching you. You can tell if they are interested or not. I never got that feeling from Susan at either audition. Yet, I felt very confident about what I was doing. *Must go into this fresh.* Each audition has to have a brand-new approach. Sure you keep things you've learned in the past, things that work for you, songs you like. But I always try to do a little something different. Even if it's just a small change. It keeps my energy fresh and alive. Keeps me out of my head, too. Performing is about being alive and in the moment. It's not about reproducing the same performance over and over and over, although some may argue that point in view of the fact that Broadway shows are performed eight shows a week. It can go there, but that's what I try to avoid. I start by treating my auditions in the same manner as my performance. Keep it fresh. Sing a song I haven't sung in a while or ever before. If I have to do a monologue I try the ones that I don't know as well. I know it sounds crazy, but it works for me. I audition better when I have to rely a little on instinct.

SUNDAY, AUGUST 20:

The audition is Tuesday. Tara Rubin called me and I threw it over to Ann, my new agent. We have to dance first and then have a song and funny story or joke ready. A joke . . . Okay. Not sure exactly how that is going to show how funny I am. I'm not a great teller of jokes, but I can be funny. At least I think I can. I would rather read from the script and be funny that way. But it seems that they didn't ask for my opinion in the breakdown.

First Audition

TUESDAY, AUGUST 22:

I arrive at the new 42nd Street Studios. These were built as part of the refurbishment of 42nd Street and, boy, are they welcome! The studios are huge with tons of sunlight. There are locker rooms and showers. Everything looks clean. The coolest thing about it is there are no bad memories here. If you talk to an actor about the various audition sites around town, there will, no doubt, be a number of different reactions to said sites because of success or failure experienced there.

> PERFORMER A: I have an audition at Nola today.
> PERFORMER B: Oh God I *hate* Nola.
> PERFORMER A: I love it. I got *Jekyll and Hyde* there.
> PERFORMER B: I have *never* had a good audition in that place.
> PERFORMER A: How many times have you been there?
> PERFORMER B: . . . Once.
> PERFORMER A: What show?
> PERFORMER B: . . . *Jekyll and Hyde.*

These new studios have no bad karma in them. That definitely helps "keep it fresh."

Anyway, I find myself outside of the dance studio with all the "regulars." Guys who I always see at auditions. We are the chorus boys. (And as much as I appreciate all the wonderful things I've learned being in the chorus, it is a group I am looking forward to graduating from sometime in the near future.) For a moment, my mind flashes to the ultra-hysterical audition scene from the movie. All the Hitler auditionees, yelling and screaming and jumping around. Perhaps I should have dressed up as Hitler?

The girls are inside finishing up their call. You really aren't supposed to watch, but most people do. People watch and try to learn the combination beforehand. I don't like to do that. I may glimpse to see what muscles I need to spend extra time warming up but I won't try to learn the steps. It's just a personal preference of mine. The buzz in the hallway starts. Seems that there are four counts at the end of the combination that Susan has asked the girls to "do something funny." One of the guys is standing at the door and is reporting everything he's seeing.

"PEEPING" TOM: "Oh my God, she's making them do an improv at the end. I *hate* improv. I can never do think of anything. . . . Oh my God, guys look at this! Susie just did a back bend and "sieg heiled" through her legs!! . . . It looks like she's asking them questions now. She's writing things down. I think she's asking for special skills. . . . Oh my God, Jen just belched on cue!"

The girls make their way out looking sweaty and exhausted. Vinnie Liff, the casting director, calls out the names of the women that have to stay and sing. (That's a callback and that's good.) The guys and I just sit and wait. The call was for 2:00; it's now 2:20. Oh well, nothing better to do, right?

The last girl comes out and now it's our turn. Susan introduces herself and her assistant, Warren Carlyle. He is a tall, thin drink of water from England. He will be teaching the combination. The choreography is a little bit of everything. It starts with a traveling time step and then goes everywhere. Turns, leaps, some tricky steps. Lots of heil's and swastika port de bras and stuff. She is trying to see what kind of dancers we are. Where our strengths and weaknesses are. The combination feels good on me. Which is a good sign. Sure enough, at the end she wants us to do four counts of our own thing. Everybody was doing splits and backbends and turns. I decide to do a big old Donald O'Connor kick-out pratfall. I don't practice it, so as not to give it away. You have to surprise them. Warren splits us into groups of four. My group is somewhere in the middle of the pack. That's fine by me. I only hate being *first*. The guys who go first *always* get the short end of the deal. Every group does it twice through. I get to the end of my first time through, I do my pratfall, make a huge thud on the ground, and every head in the room looks at me. A couple of people look worried. I start to play embarrassed that I fell. Susan and

Warren were a bit shocked, but cautiously smiling. Warren said, "You okay?" I said, "Sure." As I got up, I buckled my knee for emphasis. After our round robin Stro comes to us one by one and asks what special skills we have. Special skills may include gymnastics, baton twirling, pratfalls, juggling, cane and hat tricks, etc. The cool thing about Susan is she will ask you to do it right there, so you better not bullshit. She gets to me and I say, "Pratfalls." She says with a smile, "Riiiight." "I also do hat and cane tricks." She says, "Good." One guy did a takeoff on Molly Shannon's Catholic schoolgirl character from SNL and proceeded to do a monologue complete with a whispered "Superstar!" at the end. By the end, Susan's eyes were wide open, with her notepad over half her face. I assume she was masking the fact that her mouth was gaping wide open. She shouldn't have been so ashamed; we all looked the same way. I wasn't sure if he was brilliant or crazy. It clearly made everyone a bit uncomfortable. We all got sent back out into the hallway. Vinnie Liff came out. This is what I heard.

VINNIE: You guys are all so great. I just want to tell you that. This is such a special project we wish we could have you all. But we have to make a cut now. I need the following guys to stay. You're going to be singing. You will not be dancing anymore. If I don't call your name, thank you so much. Blah-blah-blah-blah-blah-blah-blah-blah Jeffry Denman blah-blah-blah-blah-blah-blah.

I go in to sing. This is my favorite part. They said they wanted standard music theater, so I'm singing "I've Confessed to the Breeze" from *No, No Nanette*. It's one of my favorite songs, and it's so simple and pure. I finish. Susan says, "Very nice." The music director asks me about my top. I tell him I'm a tenor. A's and B's. Then, Susan asks for my funny story.

CAUTION: *Funny Story Ahead!*

I was in high school choir practice. We were in the midst of learning a Disney medley. The song we were stuck on was "Chim Chim Cheree," from Mary Poppins. Part of the lyric goes, "Or blow me a kiss and that's lucky too." The sopranos were not doing well, and our choir director was getting upset. He then went down the row to see who knew the notes and who didn't. He always did this quickly and moved to the next person with great speed so as not to waste time. "Or blow me a kiss and that's lucky too," Good, next girl, "Or blow me a kiss . . ." etc, etc. So you had to be on his rhythm and ready when he got to you. Otherwise you'd get yelled at. And he could yell. He made football players cry. One of the girls was so nervous and scared, she was on the verge of tears. He finally got to her and she clammed up. She tried to get on his rhythm and she couldn't. She looked confused while he was getting madder and madder. Finally he screamed at her, "Sing 'or blow me'! Sing 'or blow me'!"

Susan is shocked (or is pretending to be shocked) and tries to mask her amusement. The rest of those at the table, especially Vinnie Liff, are all laughing. They're pleased, that is definite. It couldn't have gone much better than that.

The story is true. My music director in high school, Jim Deiotte, is the culprit. To this day he doesn't realize what he said, and that's the funniest part about it. I have a feeling I'll tell him someday. (Guess I just have.) Jim is the man responsible for teaching me to sing and appreciate music. He was my first mentor in musical theater back in Buffalo. Lynne Kurdziel-Formato, also a teacher in Buffalo, was my second. She taught me how to dance. I have two sets of parents: my real parents and my musical theater parents.

Between shows, Ann calls. In her wonderfully smoky and husky voice she says,

ANN: Hello my dear!
(I can already tell that I have a callback, just by the tone of her voice.)
ANN: You have a callback for *The Produuucers*!
ME: That's great! Dancing? Singing?
ANN: Yes on both. But this time they want a funny *song*.
ME: I don't have funny songs in my book.
ANN: Okay. Let's get working on that then. I'll see what I have here.
ME: I'll come in tomorrow and we can brainstorm?
ANN: Mel Brooks is going to be at the callback.
ME: Ah ha. Do I have to do the funny story again?
ANN: No! Susan wants a *joke*. No stories.
ME: Aw, but they loved my story.
ANN: Tara was adamant about it.
ME: Great. Okay, at least I got a callback. I feel good about this.
ANN: Good. Me too. I'll see you tomorrow?
ME: Yep.

When I was in *How to Succeed*, one of the cast members, Randl Ask, talked about his audition. He ran around the room singing a crazy high-speed version of "I Met a Girl" from *Bells Are Ringing* and proceeded to jump on top of the table, throwing everybody else's headshots and resumés everywhere. And what? Got the job.

What would *he* do? At dinner it hits me. I'm going to sing "I'm Super" from *South Park: Bigger, Longer, and Uncut*. A character named Big Gay Al sings it in the movie. The song talks about how a war is going on but Al is happy because he's gay and "everything's super" when you're gay. It's about as politically incorrect as you can get. It's also a big, brash Broadway show tune. My twist is that I'm going to sing it *as Hitler*. Gay Hitler. (I had no idea that Mel Brooks would be planning the same thing for the musical. If you don't know what I'm talking about, all will be revealed.) I've got a week to the audition but my mom is coming in with my Aunt Libby on Saturday, so I *really* have three days. Plenty of time. I went to Colony Music — the singers' indispensable sheet music store — between shows, got the song, and I'm in plotting mode. My girlfriend Melissa is shocked and amazed at what I plan to do. She just stands back and watches as I go to work. I'm sure she's thinking, "Who the hell am I dating?"

SATURDAY, AUGUST 26:

I ask my mom and Aunt Libby if they want to see what I plan on doing. It'll be good for me to do it for someone before the audition. I clear out my living room, get my props ready, and put the music on. They get a real charge out of it. My mom can't believe I'm going to go in and do all this. She asks me if all auditions are like this. I tell her that this is definitely an exception.

THE CALLBACK

MONDAY, AUGUST 28:

Callback mode. Up early (mainly because I couldn't sleep) and I had to see Mom and Aunt Libby off. Breakfast and Tae Bo video to get the blood moving. I hate getting to the audition too early. You just sit around and talk and lose your focus. I also don't like getting there too late because you run the risk of being frazzled and not having enough time to get settled and relaxed. Usually I get to the site about twenty minutes before and then find a different floor to hang out on or a place to be by myself. The dance is still in my body. I ran it a couple of times at the theater. I wonder if Susan is going to add on or change or anything. Gotta eat. See ya.

I tend not to look at the audition objectively so as not to get overly excited and lose focus. I truly believe that when you are auditioning, you are putting on a show. You are saying, "I am right for your show." Whether you know that or not. Most times you don't. So you have to pretend to a certain extent. Not only at the audition but before and afterward and when you wake up and when you go to bed. It's intense mental focus. That takes energy. My friends know that when I'm auditioning, I don't talk about it at all. I keep my energy focused on the task. That's why I hate when you have an audition and it goes well, but the callback isn't for another month. That's too much time to hold on to that energy and focus. I do best when it's a week or so between. But that's just me.

Susan starts by introducing Mel Brooks to all of us. This is freaky. He stands in front of us and says, "Thank you so much for being here. We wish we could hire all of you," and everybody laughed. And then everyone says to themselves, "Can't you?" Memories of watching *High Anxiety* and *Blazing Saddles* with my dad went flying through my head. Brooks's voice is so gravelly now. He talks in a shouted whisper. It seems to make him even funnier. I don't think it's hitting me that this is *the* Mel Brooks. I don't think my brain is allowing me to comprehend that. I'm too focused on the audition.

First, I danced. Danced and concentrated on trying to be funny for Mr. Brooks. Made the cut. Now I'm really nervous.

All of my props are in a bag. I've checked it a million times.

Melissa also got a callback from her previous *Producers* audition, so she and the other girls start to show up. I went in to sing. Unbeknownst to me, Melissa is watching through a window. I had changed from my dance clothes to a brown shirt and khaki pants. I immediately go over to the pianist and show him the song and how I need it played. I tell him to wait for my signal. As I take center, I politely ask Susan and the rest of the auditioners to close their eyes. They laugh and proceed to do so. I whip out my spray bottle, spritz my hair wet, comb it over in the stylish Hitler fashion, slap on a small black moustache, open my newspaper, which reads "Hitler Bombs London," and cover myself as if I were reading it. I say, "Okay" and the music starts. They laugh at the headline. I pull the paper down, and they laugh again at my Hitler guise. I started to sing. The beginning of the song is slow and sentimental even though the lyrics are about war and destruction. Then it catapults into a big show tune. I'm singing about how super I am and how cute I look in the hat I'm wearing. I jump around the room dancing and prancing, doing goose steps, hat tricks — everything I could think of. Well, they loved it.

I find Melissa after I come out. She tells me that Susan's jaw was on the floor during the entire song and that Mel was laughing hysterically. It was such a rush for me that I don't remember any of it. I only know that my heart was racing a million miles a minute. I had never done anything like that before and wondered if I was going to be able to carry it off. Now I know I can.

They ask me to learn some lines from the script (called "sides"). Three characters: a gay choreographer, a prison guard, and a Hitler auditionee (how apropos).

I had Mel laughing a couple of times, especially during the gay choreographer bit. (How did I have the nerve to audition for this man?) They ask me to sing a little "Springtime for Hitler," which I don't know well. Yes, I'm a fan of the film, but I haven't watched it in years. Much less sat down and tried to learn "Springtime." Who knew I'd ever have to actually sing it? The accompanist plays it through once for me. I sight-read it as best I can but before I'm ready they want me to perform it. I need one more time through but it looks like I'm not going to get it. I sing it. I didn't nail it. But they've apparently heard enough. As I exit, Tara tells me not to leave. After the rest of the guys go in and sing, they call four guys in — James Hadley, Abe Sylvia, another guy whose name I don't remember, and me. Susan and what seemed like hundreds of people behind the table stare at us for about three minutes. Halfway through, Susan says, "We're sorry we have to do this to you but it's really about a certain look." I want to say, "Hey, I got no problem. I could be outside *wishing* I were in here. Stare at me all you want." But of course I don't. Then, that's it. They let us go without another word. We exited the room feeling the stares of the guys around us. I hear friends of mine say, "You got it man, you got it." But I don't believe it. I never believe it until the offer comes.

CATS, BACKSTAGE

WEDNESDAY, AUGUST 30:

I've just finished the first show and I'm getting ready to get some dinner before the second, when my cell phone rings.

> ANN: Hellooo there!
>> (See? She's so easy to read.)
> ANN: They want you for the ensemble! Congratulations!
> ME: That's great. Thank you. Any word about understudies or specialties?
> ANN: No. Did you read for any at the callback?

ME: Yeah, I read for a gay choreographer, a prison guard, and a Hitler auditionee. They liked what I did.

ANN: That's good. Tara said all specialties will be given out in rehearsal. We'll have to wait.

ME: Can you ask her about the Matthew cover?

ANN: Yes.

Holy shit, do I feel great! I want to scream. But I don't. Dennis would be proud. "Sign your contract in your dressing room." I go to James Hadley's room (we promised each other that we would tell the other when we heard something) and ask if he's heard. He hasn't. I assure him he will. He congratulates me. I feel like shit for having opened my big mouth. After talking to James I run to Melissa's dressing room. She's ecstatic. I try not to make a big deal out of it. There are a lot of different personalities at the theater, and there is no need for me to go overboard. Some of the cast members are feeling a bit anxious about the show closing. The last thing they need to hear is my news. So I scream when the subway cars are passing.

The relief, and the excitement, and the new prospects — they all overwhelm me. I can't stop thinking about it all day and night. What's going to happen? What will I be doing? Will it be good? The rehearsals don't start until December 4, more than three months away. Will I make it until then?

Time to Put the Cat to Sleep

THURSDAY, SEPTEMBER 7:

We're getting ready for the big night. It doesn't seem real. It's going to be very weird to perform *Cats* for the last time on Broadway. At least this incarnation. Watch the Dodgers revive it in 2010. (The Dodgers produced *How to Succeed* and tend to specialize in revivals.) My parents will be coming in, as will Melissa's. I love that I can do this for my parents. It makes me happy to show them where life can take them and me. They deserve it. They sacrificed a lot of "living" so that we — my brothers Bob and Gregg and myself — could have what we have. I don't think I could ever repay that.

SATURDAY, SEPTEMBER 9:

The producers threw a brunch today at the Marriott Marquis for all the companies of the *Cats* tour and the Broadway show. It was cool. The best part was when Marlene Danielle (the only remaining original cast member) came over and told me that Harry Groener was at the party. He made it! I had wanted him to see me ever since I got the job.

Harry Groener

In 1992 I visited New York and saw *Crazy for You.* The show had quite an impact on me. Not only did it introduce me to Susan Stroman's work but I discovered Harry Groener. He starred in the show. At the time, I fancied myself quite the young song-and-dance man. (Still do.) In *Crazy for You*, Harry was brilliant. I instantly became an admirer. I began researching other shows he had done and found him on the TV sitcom *Dear John.* Fast-forward to the summer of 1999. I was understudying Harry in *If Love Were All* at the Lucille Lortel Theatre. That's when I first auditioned for *Cats.* Harry was playing Noel Coward opposite Twiggy's Gertrude Lawrence. Before I went to the callback for *Cats* I went into his dressing room and told him I was up for Munkustrap, the role he created. He was excited and sent good vibes my way. When I got it, all I wanted was for him to see me, never thinking that I would be the last Munk. So there's something poetic for me that he was the first and I am the last. The universe is strange and surprising that way.

Melissa and I didn't know a heck of a lot of people at the brunch, so we roamed around and said hi to those we did know. The feeling around the room was so moving and supportive. I say that because ever since I joined *Cats* I have gotten the fish-eye from most theater people — even from some friends. ("Oh, you're doing *Cats*? Wow, that's . . . great, Jeff.") I think people in our business forget what shows mean to us when we first hear or see them as kids, that first reaction to a cast recording, the feeling that the people on that recording are eternal. I didn't know anything about performing when I first listened to *Cats*. I never dreamed that I could be playing the role of Munk on Broadway, much less be in the final cast. That I could, in my own way, become "eternal," as Harry had become to me. That meant something to me. And ever since I had joined the cast, I desperately wanted *Cats* to enjoy some of the respect it had had in its youth. And if our closing weekend did nothing else, it did that. It let us all revel in the fact that this was, in its own way, a great show. I maintain that *Cats* was always better for the actors who had done it than for the actors who had seen it. An actor out front saw the flaws, the inconsistencies, the strings. An actor onstage became part of the tribe. Even if some actors finally became jaded, many were won over by their own imaginations. That's worth watching.

Saturday Matinee — U.S. Tours Invite

This weekend (two shows Saturday, one show Sunday) the shows are all by invitation only. This makes it even more special for us. This afternoon the theater shook with the sound of eighteen hundred former *Cats*. The casts from the American tours were invited to the matinee. They gave us a performance we will never forget.

It almost felt like a pep rally. Perhaps that's just what it was, a rally for the final homecoming. The seniors are graduating and everyone feels time slipping away. Sometimes the personal moments (as opposed to actions dictated by specific choreography or direction), we had created seemed to go unnoticed, but today they were doubly noticed by those eagle-eyed watchers. It's strange to do a performance for a theater full of people who know the show as well as you do. They laughed at all our bits and cheered at all our tricks. I only fear that closing night will not be as big.

THE CLOSING

SUNDAY, SEPTEMBER 10:

Morning

The parents are in. Very excited. Mom is already dreading not seeing the big cat eyes on Broadway and 50th. She loves the show, always has.

> MOM: You know something Jeffry? When you first moved here and you lived on 50th and 9th, we'd pass by the theater and I'd say a novena so that you would be in *Cats* someday.

How's that for the power of prayer?

The whole day seems unreal. My parents are a welcome distraction. Today is one of those days when you can say that you've achieved or acquired something in your lifetime that no one can ever take away. Athletes talk about championships that way. "No matter what else happens in your life you can always say that . . ." Me, I'm honored to say that I was in the final cast of *Cats*. I respect *Cats* for what it was and what it meant to a lot of people. To be a part of that, to have the honor of telling the last stories it had to tell, is something I will always cherish.

The Show

It's 4:00 and we're at the theater. It feels different. Backstage, the house, the dressing rooms. There is a low hum of excitement buzzing. Everyone has this glaze over their eyes, as if imagining something very intensely. John, the doorman — our King of the Understatement — says, "Well, this is it!" OB (David O'Brien, the production supervisor and head stage manager) stops me on the stairs.

OB: Hey Jeffry, when you get a chance, they've installed some additional fog machines behind the tire for the "Heaviside Layer" moment. They want Grizabella's tire to be completely enveloped in fog. Take a look before the show, okay?
ME: Oh, sure, *Now* they spend the money for more fog. Where were they a year ago?"

Final night gifts are a tradition. I passed out my gifts and cards to everyone. My parents wanted to watch me do my makeup one last time. The makeup is still one of my favorite parts of the process. Dad took pictures.

This is like the last day of school. As a child, I remember feeling a sense of excitement that the school year was over, but at the same time a fear that things were going to be different from what I had gotten used to. In kindergarten I had a child-level traumatic experience when Mrs. Valentine, my favorite teacher up to that point in my life, said that she wasn't going to be our teacher the following year. I didn't get it. I didn't like it. And when I get close to people and get used to having them around, there's a part

My last meow.

of me that gets upset that any "Mrs. Valentine" isn't going to be there in the same way. I walked around the theater with that very same feeling. We were never going to be together in this way again. I wonder what Millie is going to do. I wonder what "Rocky" is going to do. Millie and Rocky are two of the wardrobe people who have been there the longest. I know they'll be fine, but I also know that I won't see them on a regular basis if at all. They may retire after this. They both deserve it.

OB calls "half hour." My parents head out to get a cup of coffee before the show, I get into costume and make my usual rounds. I make sure to visit all the dressing rooms before the show starts. Everybody is happy and sad at the same time. Well, not everybody. Some are just sad. Some are just happy. A few are really happy. Not *happy*, happy. *Angrily*, happy. Like, "I'm glad this fucking show is closing so I can get on with my life." "Well," I think, "you could always have gone on with your life. No one was twisting your arm to be here. Plus, who wants you to be here if you don't? Not me." They were just relieved, I guess. Good for them.

OB calls "places" for the last time, and I remember that I hadn't checked the new fog machines that he told me about. Oh, well. I have some time before I make my entrance; I'll do it then.

The overture starts and the crowd goes crazy. Even louder than the Saturday matinee. Everyone puts on their "flashing green eyes" and gets ready to try to scare the audience. Of course, they all know what's coming. The overture continues and gives us our cue. The first pair of eyes gleam in the darkness and the audience erupts. Almost deafening. As I shine my flashing eyes into the faces of the crowd, I see expressions of excitement and happiness I had seldom seen before. Every person is smiling. Usually during "Green Eyes," you might get one or two audience members who were excited to see you, but others might be bored or pissed that you startled them. But not this evening. Not this performance.

After "Green Eyes" I get behind the tire and I see what OB was talking about. And I realize why these hadn't been put here before. The fog machines are huge, like a big black washing machine with an enormous hose rising up into the air. With all of the rest of the garbage in the *Cats'* junkyard, they fit right in.

As Munk, I have the first line in the opening number. From the first day of rehearsal, I was told to make the audience uncomfortable by waiting. "Make them go crazy with anticipation," OB would tell me. So tonight, I wait and wait and wait and wait before I sing it. Everyone knew it was coming. Everyone knew exactly what I was going to say. I saw that first line as being the point of no return. Once I say it, the show will begin. The end had to begin. So I say it. And the end begins.

As each cat enters and sings their solo, cheers erupt from various parts of the audience. When she enters, Marlene gets an ovation worthy of the time she has spent here. Chills.

During the "Choir on the Tire" moment, I hear sniffles and choked up breaths from behind me. A strange thing about me: when an emotional moment hits me, and tears should be next, I laugh. My diaphragm pulls up and jerks around and makes me laugh. Happens when I'm watching a good movie or hearing a sad song. I laugh all the way through "Choir on the Tire."

At the end of the opening number, John Dewar and I approach the audience and ask someone what a Jellicle Cat is. So here I am, asking this audience filled with people who *know* what a Jellicle cat is, "Do I actually see with my own very eyes, a man who's not heard of a Jellicle cat?" They laugh hysterically. They're right with me. The first time that lyric ever became ironic. Lovely.

I have closed shows before. Indeed, people make fun of the fact that every Broadway show I've gotten — *How to Succeed*, *Dream*, and now *Cats* — has closed while I was in it. During final performances, the thought constantly goes through my head, "I will never do this again." "I will never do that again." Tonight is no different. I watch as the moments and the choreography and the lines fly by, and I say a quick farewell to them. Eighteen years had come down to this performance with these cast members. I am having a Fierce Moment.

A Primer on Fierce Moments

A Fierce Moment is the creation of three friends of mine, Dennis Stowe, Jon Erik Parker, and Capathia Jenkins. It's very simple. You find yourself in a situation that is exceptional. The universe is clicking for you. You have a constant state of chills and find yourself saying (either aloud or silently), "This is so cool." That is a Fierce Moment. We've all had them. What Dennis, Jon Erik, and Capathia do in this moment is call attention to it. They will announce it, raise a toast, or even pick up a phone and call up one another to let them know that one is occurring. It's a marvelous way of enjoying, appreciating, and living your life in the moment.

We get to the end of the first act riding the highs from the opening, and we start the Jellicle Ball. We all know this is going to be the one where they go insane. Eighteen years of doing that fifteen-minute dance from hell. Doing *Cats* was about getting through the Jellicle Ball. And everyone in that audience knew it. So we begin and the audience starts to crackle. They know what we're thinking, they know which of our body parts were starting to hurt, and they probably feel their own, aching in their seats. We get to the "sensual" section, where all the cats crawl into a writhing clump at the center of the stage. After the "sensual" section, there is a Grizabella "scare," which sends us into the "buildup" before the huge, full-company "Copland" section. (These were the names that Gillian Lynne, the show's choreographer, gave to the various parts of the ball. I don't know where she got them from.) As the "buildup" section climaxes, we hear someone scream from the audience, "GO FOR IT!!!" We scream, then the audience screams, and the music and the dancing explode together.

In the final movement of the ball, all the *Cats* are gathered on the tire around Old Deut. They twirl and spin and flip and run and dance straight at the audience as the music rises and climaxes into two final hits. Most of the cats end in some sort of kneeling or lying position on the floor, reaching out to the audience. Munk ends in a kneeling back arch, which, under normal circumstances, I could hold for quite a while before breaking and moving on to "Little Memory." Well. The audience is going nuts as we finish the ball, and we were told not to break too soon by stage management. Ben, the conductor, would be given the signal to start up again. So we fix our eyes on him. The applause goes

on and on and on and on and on. (Later, OB said that it was exactly 1 minute, 42 seconds. That doesn't sound like a lot of time,
but onstage it's enormous.) We all hold our positions. Of course,
my abs are killing me, as are my arms. I have to reset my arm position twice. Every time I reset, the audience cheers louder. A
blanket of applause and cheers. I can feel my heart beating faster
and faster, as if it's trying to match the chanting and the vibra-
tions of the crowd. I start to laugh.

During intermission I hear that Susan Stroman is in the audience. It's a rumor, I thought, but people were swearing that she
was there. I don't need any incentive to do my best tonight. I'm
proud of what I have done with Munk. If she's out there, I'm glad
she's getting a chance to see me perform before we work together.

At our final bows, the audience goes crazy. The swings and the
orchestra and the stage management staff come out onstage with
us. The principals (Jimmy Lockett, Steve Bienskie, Marlene,
Linda Balgord, Julius Sermonia, John Dewar, and I) go out into
the audience and round up the notables: Sir Andrew Lloyd Web-
ber, Gerald Schoenfeld, and Phillip Smith of the Shuberts. I look
over at my parents, sitting in the second row and snapping away
with the camera. Gerald Schoenfeld is the first to speak. He tells
about the business end of the production, about how *Cats* saved
the road business, and he thanks the creative types who brought
it from London. It was such a huge success that Broadway tour-
ing was revived. It did the same for Broadway in her leanest years,
with both the New York and the road companies employing tens
of thousands of people. Never thought about it that way. Sir Andrew is next and he mentions that he "doesn't know what all the
fuss is about." This is only the first of *Cats'* nine lives, according
to him. (A subconscious groan goes through the cast and audience. Don't start talking about revivals on closing night.) He continues telling us how much of a risk *Cats* was in London when it

was conceived and asks that Broadway keep taking risks. He introduces Trevor Nunn, Cameron Mackintosh, and Gillian Lynne. Gillian gives hugs and kisses all around as she comes up.

Trevor and Cameron both spoke eloquently and succinctly about how much *Cats* changed their lives. I was disappointed that Gillian didn't get to say anything. So much of what gave *Cats* its life was what she did. She was there through the years, coming back and working with the various casts. Seems to me that she deserved a moment for herself.

Stephen Bienskie (Rum Tum Tugger) screams his final line to finish the evening, and to our thrill and surprise, confetti machines start blowing yellow and black and silver confetti from every corner of the theater. These were the machines OB had told us were for "more fog." Bienskie and I scream like little girls and then laugh at our reaction. In seconds we are in a wall of confetti, unable to see anything.

As it clears I find Melissa, Dennis, and my parents. They snap

Cats and confetti. *Me and Stephen Bienskie onstage.*

pictures of us. I kiss them and hug them. Vinnie Liff, who was sitting in front of my parents, got kisses and hugs from me as well. Onstage the entire cast is congratulating each other and hugging and crying. Even the people who had been so angrily happy a few hours ago had tears in their eyes. Universal joy and sadness in everyone's eyes.

The Party

I send my parents ahead to the party and get myself showered and changed. Once dressed I join a small fashion show the men are having, to see what we're all wearing. Now everyone is intent on getting onto the shuttle buses and getting to the party. I stop by Melissa's dressing room. Not ready. I'm surprised. She's usually very quick. So I go downstairs and outside to get some air and see that some of the fans are still here. There are police barricades up and the fans are lined up around them. I sign some autographs and say hello to some of the diehards who had come so many

Best Friends. *Me, Dennis Stowe, and Melissa at the Closing Night party.*

times before but couldn't get tickets to the closing. A woman from *People* magazine asks if she can interview me. I figure I have the time. After about fifteen minutes with her, I go back inside. The girls still aren't ready. I start singing "Waiting for the Girls Upstairs" from *Follies*. Finally they come down and they shuffle onto the shuttle bus, looking gorgeous, and we head to the party for the fireworks. As we turn onto the West Side Highway I look into the distance and see the fireworks start to go off. They look magnificent.

The party is at Pier 61 inside Chelsea Piers, New York's massive recreation complex. Melissa and I find our parents and Dennis in the main hall and then go out to the boat to have some dinner. Harry Groener and his wife, Dawn, are there. After I introduce everyone, Harry says the most wonderful things to my parents about working with me. We sit down and start eating together. I couldn't have planned it better. During dinner Cynthia Tornquist from CNN passes by and interviews Melissa and me. My parents beam and constantly look over at me, smiling, still reeling from the performance.

Later on in the evening, I introduce myself to Michael Riedel, the theater "gossip" writer for the *New York Post*, whom I had come to dislike after he wrote some scathing columns about *Dream*. I am curious to see what he could possibly say to a performer in the final cast of a show that he (probably) hates. He tells me that he's also from western New York — Rochester. He had enjoyed the evening thoroughly, admiring the talent of the cast. Maybe he's not so bad after all. We're so fickle, we actors. Give us a compliment and we're yours. He asks if I have anything in the works. I tell him about *The Producers*. He says to me with a sarcastic tone: "I can't *wait* to see that. Has all the makings of a floperoo." I nod and say, "Yeah, I guess we'll see." I mean, really, what was I supposed to say? I have no idea what it's going to be like and no one else does, either. He mentions that Mel Brooks is writing the songs, and that he doesn't have a lot of faith in that. I am a firm believer in karma and that what you put out will get around to you. So I half-nod and take a drink of my Jack and Coke, thinking, "Yeah, what the heck have I gotten myself into?"

Melissa and I introduce ourselves to Terrence Mann and Betty Buckley. I thank them for making such indelible impressions on my performer's psyche. They enjoyed the show greatly and had some wonderful things to say. Memories of me on my living room floor listening to the cast recording for the first time raced through my head as I was talking to them. Such an opportunity! We try to find Susan Stroman, but hear that we've missed her. The orchestra playing gets the better of us and Melissa and I decide to dance a bit. My parents join us. They're the best "jitterbuggers" I know.

My parents have to leave tomorrow morning, very early, so when the crowd starts to dissolve, we make our way out and head home. My dad says to me, "You never cease to amaze us, Jeffry." My mom joins in with, "You have so many special people in your life. It's so wonderful to know that they're here for you." It does my mom good to know that I'm okay here. Hell, same for my dad. They both worried constantly when I first moved, as parents should. Used to be that my dad wouldn't stay in the city for more than a day. He'd come in, see the show that I was in because he wouldn't come in if I wasn't in a show, and then leave. Things have changed. They know I'm safe, they know the city is, for the most part, safe, and they see that I am intensely happy. And they love Melissa. That helps a great deal. I feel that evenings like this one are the way that I get to thank them for being such great parents.

A ROAD NOT TAKEN

I've been dealing with a bit of a dilemma this week. I finally came to a conclusion about it. In *Backstage* I happened to see an audition notice to perform with the Manhattan Rhythm Kings: Hal Shane, Brian Nalepka, and Tripp Hansen. I've been a fan of the Kings for a while and thought I should call. They were looking for a strong singer who dances and possibly plays an instrument. I called and set up the audition. It sounded like I was what they were looking for. Tripp Hansen was leaving the group, and they wanted someone to take over. When I got to the audition, they were all there. I did a little song and dance to "I'd Rather Lead a Band." They really liked it. I sang a little three-part with them to "Glowworm." It was great. I love singing tight harmonies, and to sing with them was a trip. Pardon the pun. They offered me the job on the spot, and I told them I needed to think about it. I hadn't told them about *The Producers* because I wanted to see what the commitment was going to be.

I went to Ann's after the audition and told her what happened. She was supportive but a bit cautious. She wanted to know what the schedule would be. How much would I be working and, most important, how much New York exposure would I be getting? If we were going to be playing the Rainbow Room and the Algonquin and a show at Carnegie Hall with Tommy Tune, that was one thing. She felt that *The Producers* was a once-in-a-lifetime event. But she never tried to tell me what to do. That ended up having a lot to do with the decision I finally made.

I called Brian and told him about *The Producers*. He put Hal Shane on, and before I could get a word out, he invited me to lunch. I had been dealing only with Brian. He's a fairly laid-back guy. Hal started the lunch meeting with, "Okay. Brian does the intros and the nice-guy stuff. *I'm* the hard sell." And, boy, was he. In the course of an hour and a half, we went from a restaurant on 72nd to Hal's apartment. He and Brian gave me the entire Kings' history. Where they came from and where they were going. They saw me as someone who fit in with what they were trying to do. For that matter, so did I. During the meeting I went from one extreme to the other. Hal challenged me and said that being a King is hard work and not for the light-hearted, but that the rewards are great. It was hard to argue with him while he showed me the pictures and awards and recordings and famous friends they've made over the years. For a second, in between two of Hal's sentences (he had to breathe at some point), I stepped outside of myself and looked at what was happening. The Manhattan Rhythm Kings wanted me as a member. It was almost too much to comprehend. Hal noticed it and started to press the issue. He was really starting to get to me. I had come to the meeting with the idea that I wasn't going to be a Rhythm King. I left his apartment with more tapes and CDs than I could carry, pamphlets on the Kings and their travels, calling Melissa on my cell phone saying, "I'm going to be a Rhythm King." She simply said, "Jeff, just come home."

I had no idea what the hell I was going to do. She was blunt as always. I told her everything that had happened and what they had said. When I relayed the story I noticed that it didn't sound as exciting as Hal had made it sound. Melissa was confused, because she, too, failed to grasp the excitement. She told me she thought it might not be the best thing for my career right now. The main point was that I would be out of work from now until March. I would be rehearsing starting in December for a cruise with Tommy Tune. That's three months of rehearsing with no pay for a week of work in March. Then, no work until May.

Once the summer hits, the gigs start to pick up. And they live like this regularly. Gigs come and gigs go, and you just make do. Sometimes you're up, sometimes you're down. I've already been there. And even though it wasn't with the Manhattan Rhythm Kings, I really don't want to go back there. I'm more interested in getting my "principal" feet in the door now. I want to do roles. Becoming a Manhattan Rhythm King, while it wouldn't hurt that, wouldn't help, either. Hal said it himself: the concert world that they travel in is a different world from theater. Melissa asked what Ann thought. I told her that she had been nothing but supportive. That's when I realized how cool Ann had been about the whole thing. I had just signed with her, and she was standing behind a decision that would take me out of any jobs that she could help me get. In a way, I wanted to thank her for being so straight up with me. So, I finally called Hal and told him that it just wasn't the right time for me. He was disappointed, but he wished me well. I hope that we can cross "performing paths" someday. Though I know I have made the right decision, I will always wonder how it might have turned out. If *The Producers* is a flop, I will wonder even more.

WEDNESDAY, OCTOBER 25:

The phone rings.

ANN: Hellooo!
ME: Hi Ann. Sounds like good news.
ANN: Tara just called. They want you to come in tomorrow and read for the Leo Bloom cover!

This is what I've wanted from Day One. This will make it worth it. I had promised myself that I wasn't going to do ensemble anymore; that I was going to hold out and do principals, even if it meant leaving New York for a bit and doing regional theater. If you have "ensemble" on your resumé, that's what casting folk see you as. They don't see potential. That would make their job too difficult. It's much easier to look at my name and say, "Oh, look, he's been a swing on two Broadway shows. He's a swing." That way they don't have to think twice. Same with the word *ensemble*. Once that's on your resumé, that's what you are, until you prove otherwise. And that's the hardest thing to do. One way to show them is to get an understudy assignment. I had understudied Matthew for a brief period during *How to Succeed*. But I never got the chance to go on for him. Matthew doesn't go out much. I want this one from the get-go. I know I can do this.

I go to Johnson-Liff and pick up the audition material. It's a huge scene. I hate that I have only a day. It's practically the entire first scene with Bialystock. There is a note in the margin saying where to start and where to stop. My instinct tells me to ignore them. Why give me the whole scene? Better that I'm familiar with all of it. I staple the lines (also called "sides") into an accounting book so that I have both a prop and my lines close, in case I need them. I don't have time to memorize the entire scene. I considered watching the movie but thought better of it. Melissa runs the scene with me a couple of times after dinner. She insists I'm ready, but I don't feel comfortable with the section where Leo reveals the "scheme." I feel like I'm trying to make it funny when all it needs to be is innocent and truthful.

LEO BLOOM UNDERSTUDY AUDITION

THURSDAY, OCTOBER 26:

I prep all day. At 6:00 I head down. I have my suit on, my glasses, and my hair done. I believe in dressing for the audition. Again, for most auditioners, I feel you have to show them that you fit the part. Key words: *show them*.

I get to Chelsea Studios about fifteen minutes before my call. I don't go through the scene because I had been through it enough at home. I know it. Better that I just relax, I figure. I go in and *everybody's* there. Richard Frankel (general manager), Mel Brooks, Susan Stroman, and countless others all face me in the way only an auditioner can. I think about the fact that our business, in its natural state, is done on a stage with the benefit of an audience, orchestra, costumes, props, lighting, even makeup. An audition consists of barely *any* of those things. That's precisely why I feel it necessary to dress up for auditions. You have to get as much in your corner as you can.

Susan comes over to me first, gives me a strong hug, and says, "Congratulations. We're so happy to have you." That helps. I remember that I have the job. Just show them what you can do. Be what they want — because that's the trick to auditioning, I feel. They want you to be perfect. They want you to walk in and be exactly what they're looking for. After I shake hands with the folks behind the tables, including Mel, I step back and ask, "Where should I start?" Susan says, "Why don't you take it from 'Ahem'?" "Ahem" is about four pages prior to where the margin notes say to "start." It's the part where Leo tries to tell Bialystock that there's a discrepancy in the books. I prep for a sec and go into the scene. Before I say a word, I act as though I'm working on the books. Then, I notice the discrepancy. I look up at the "audience," then, meekly, almost scared, look over at Max (being played by a reader). I don't know what I did, but I have the table laughing. It caught me off guard but I press on. I do the whole blue blanket breakdown section, and then Susan stops me. She stops me right where the margin notes say, "start." (Note to self: NEVER PAY ATTENTION TO NOTES ON THE SIDES. Thank God I had become familiar with the whole scene. If I had just learned what the notes said, I'd have been screwed.) Susan smiles and says, "Thanks. That was great." I'm thinking, "That's it? I don't get a second time through? There is no *way* I could have done everything you wanted. I didn't do everything *I* wanted." I call Melissa and tell her the situation. She says, "Is it possible that you did really well?" I reply, "No."

In 1998–99 I was holding auditions for my own show *Dancing in the Dark*. It was a great opportunity to see from the other side of the table. It taught me more about auditioning than I could have ever learned by staying on the actor's side. In the same vein, I thought that because I am an actor and understand that side of it, I was a very fair auditioner, giving people as much of a chance to show their best as I could. As an actor, I know that reading a scene once isn't enough. The first time, you are a jangle of nerves, trying to hit the marks you set for yourself while trying to stave off the adrenaline. The second time through, you have the benefit of a bit of relaxation. Plus, you can work off the notes the director (hopefully) gives. You can be a bit more in control and, thus, do better. As a result, you can get an idea of how well you did or did not do. At the end of this audition, Susan didn't give me any indication of how well I did or did not do. I don't know her well enough to know if "Thanks. That was great" is a true statement or just a polite signal that the audition is over. Looking back, I still have no idea. The life of an actor.

MONDAY, OCTOBER 30:

Ann has called Tara a number of times to try to get feedback. Nothing. Apparently they will be assigning understudies once we are in rehearsal. Now is the time to let this go. I can't possibly hold on to this for a month and a half. I did what I could. Done. Out of my hands.

FIRST COSTUME FITTING

THURSDAY, NOVEMBER 16:

Today is my first measurement session with the wardrobe department. I love this part. Making the costumes. This is how you learn what's happening in the show before rehearsal starts. Doug Petitjean, the wardrobe supervisor from *How to Succeed*, is there. It's great to see a friendly face, and he's glad to see me as well. The whole crew seems very fun and nice. William Ivey Long is the costume designer. He's not there, but his right hand, Martha, is and is basically in charge of the event. A blonde comes out of the dressing area. Very pretty, very young. I assume she's in the show. I catch her name, Bryn. So far, I know Angie Schworer, Tracy Terstriep, and now Bryn. I look at the cast list hanging on the wall to see if I recognize any other names. I don't. Besides Abe Sylvia, who I knew in passing at *Cats*, and Brad Musgrove, I don't know anyone else. They finish with Bryn and I enter. As I get measured and photographed (in my skivvies), I learn that the entire ensemble will be dressing up as old ladies. I ask what for. Martha says, "The Little Old Lady Walker Ballet." I start to laugh. People roll their eyes and say, "You ever done a show with Stro?" I tell them no. "Oh, just wait, she's gonna have you dancing with everything but the stage hands." I call Melissa to tell her about the Walker Ballet. She says, "This is going to be ridiculous, isn't it?" I certainly hope so.

Interior Doubt Monologue

Thoughts start to run through my head: Are they gilding the lily here? *The Producers* is such a funny movie. Can all those moments really be musicalized and be as funny? I have to think that Matthew and Nathan signing on is a sign that things are good in *script land*. But I am reminded of *Big* and *Saturday Night Fever*. Great movies, bad musicals.

FIRST DAY OF REHEARSAL

MONDAY, DECEMBER 4:

It starts today. I have no idea what is in store. Usually, my instincts kick in and give me an idea of what's in store. Emphasis on *usually*. I do know it will be an experience. Odds say it will be a good one. But I've never trusted odds. Everyone seems to think that I've got the best job of the season. Others think we (notice that it's "we" now) will be hard pressed to compete with the memory of the movie. I fall into that category. I couldn't sleep at all. I got out of bed at 6:30 and made breakfast. It's like the first day of school. Every time you start a new show. That's part of what I love about this business. Meeting a new group of people who will be family in no time. I can't sit anymore.

I get to the rehearsal hall (the new 42nd Street studios) and meet Ira Mont, one of the stage managers. He gives me a combination for a locker downstairs. A locker? I get a locker? This is bizarre. Usually, the perimeter of a rehearsal hall is filled with dance bags and coats (especially in winter) and all manner of things, actor-related. But here we get to put our stuff in a locker. That's a good sign. The rehearsal room is big and bright, lots of windows, although it doesn't seem big enough for a Broadway show. I've always rehearsed at 890 Broadway, which is where all the shows used to rehearse. Now they're all over the place. But the 42nd Street studios are new. It's nice to rehearse a Broadway show near Broadway.

I give my body a stretch. People start roaming in. Matt Loehr and Eric Gunhus came in about the same time I did. Matt knows me from *Cats*. Congratulates me on the final show; he was there. Eric, I assume, is the guy who will be singing "Springtime." He's a classic Aryan. Tall, good-looking, blond hair, blue eyes. With a name like Gunhus, how can you go wrong? The schedule says that we will be singing first today. That's pretty standard.

So today and the rest of the week, it's just the ensemble. Stro wants to get the big numbers out of the way. We start singing and I'm very impressed with the music. This is what I've been waiting to see: how Mel is as a composer. The first song is "Op'ning Night," the top of the show. Apparently the show starts outside the Shubert at Bialystock's latest flop, *Funny Boy* (the musical version of *Hamlet*; I'm already laughing). The lyrics are hysterical and the music is good old standard Broadway. It sounds like a million Broadway opening numbers but still fresh and new. I've always dreamed of singing the word *shit* in an opening number. We move to a *Fiddler*-esque song that Max sings called "King of Broadway." I am playing the "Blind Violinist." I get to say, "It's good to be the king" — Mel's line from *History of the World: Part I*. Then we move to the granddaddy of them all. "Springtime." I'm a Bavarian peasant in the beginning, then a tapping storm trooper. I hear I will be playing FDR in the "Challenge Tap" section. *That* I cannot wait for. FDR will be in a wheelchair. Could be *very* funny. But I don't want to get my hopes up. Patrick Brady is the musical director. I really like his work. He knows exactly what he wants. He knows the score inside out. Jim Deiotte would be proud. Musical directors like him make me want to work harder. I like knowing that the people in charge are prepared and know their shit.

Lunch happens. A bunch of us go across the street to the food court. I'm frightened as I ride the escalator up. Suddenly you are no longer in the warm confines of old dilapidated theaters and the Port Authority. Now, you have been thrust, by way of an escalator, into something sparkling clean, sterile, and characteristically un–New York. It makes me cringe. I came to New York because of its history, its character, and its peccadilloes. The last thing I ever wanted to see was an Applebee's sign floating above 42nd Street. I'm sure Middle America loves it. Makes them feel they never left home. Mind you, I support the refurbishment of the area. I just wish the architects could have avoided the whole Lego and Erector Set design that the street now displays so garishly. Thank God the movie theaters tried to maintain some semblance of what had been there before. Anyway. I overcome my nausea so that I can eat a bite or two before I go back.

After lunch we start working on "Springtime." The beginning is good ole happy peasant stuff. Kathy Fitzgerald and I immediately start screwing around. At one point we have to sing, "Where, oh where, was he?" — meaning Hitler. Stro wants us to pantomime looking for something. She tells us that she wants it to look like bad choreography. So I look at Kathy and her ample bosom, which she is clearly proud of, and say, "I'm going to look in your cleavage." She laughs and says, "That's great. Go for it." So we do. It gets kept. Only problem is we can't do it without laughing. After the peasant section, we all have to exit. Stro gives us how many counts we have, and she says, "Just exit, but make it fun." So everybody starts trying to come up with stuff. I look at Jennifer Smith, one of the other character women, and she's looking at me. Practically at the same time we say, "Lift?" We work out a crappy lift that only the worst choreographer would set, and Stro loves it. Everybody came up with funny stuff. We watch everyone's bits, one at a time, and have a good laugh.

After Bavaria we move on to the entrance of the "Follies girls." Hard to get an idea of what this is going to look like without their costumes. We have been told that they will be somewhat like they are in the movie. One girl will be sausage, one beer, one Valkyrie, and one pretzel. Then we have to get the tap shoes out. The tapping is basic and fun. We have some swastika arms and legs stuff that is difficult to get a handle on. On breaks, everyone is flailing about, including myself. Robert Fowler and I start to hit it off. He knows my friend Dennis. Abe and Matt seem to be more *dancer dancers* than Robert and I, so we bond through that. The tapping storm trooper section starts with what we learned at the audition. Lots of heil-ing, dropping grenades, and cheesy smiles. Warren Carlyle is Stro's right-hand man, and he's a really lovely guy. Very supportive and helpful, but a bit of a taskmaster. We go beyond my threshold of stamina. I remember that I've been out of work for two months. I don't mind getting back into shape, I'm just worried about the body tomorrow morning. By the end of the day we have a nice-sized chunk done. We sound great as an ensemble. Kudos to Stro and Patrick Brady. It's an underappreciated talent, I think, to audition people separately and find folks who not only can do what you need in the show but also make a good blend vocally. Not everyone knows how to sing in a chorus. It's harder than singing solo.

Dancer Boy Number Two

The lines have been drawn very clearly as to who is a "character man" and who is a "singer-dancer." It's the ever-present caste system of theater. A character man is "closer" to a principal than a singer-dancer is. So they think, "Well, at least I'm not the bottom rung." Unspoken rules start to apply. This will become even more apparent down the road, when the bows are set and when dressing room assignments are given. I've seen principals (and not necessarily stars), not talk to anyone who doesn't have a line.

It's ridiculous. In this show, the creative team has set this up very clearly. Usually the actors figure it out themselves beforehand. But we all had been given so little info that we don't know what we're going to be doing. But *they* know. Half of me hates that and the other half sees the need. The part that hates it feels, "Don't pigeonhole me before you know what I can do. And don't think you know what I can do from my audition. That's only part of what I can do." On the other hand, in the first few days of any show I've ever been involved in, everyone scrambles to make sure that they are going to get good bits and be seen by their mom and not be upstaged. Add to that the fact that everyone wants a shot at making Mel Brooks laugh, and you have an idea of what kind of chaos the creative team can be dealing with. They have collected a group of people who all want to be funny. All you need is one person to start it, then everybody feels they have to scramble to be seen or else they won't get anything good, and you have egos and bad feelings, blah, blah, blah. At the bottom of this is the fact that, for the most part, actors are incredibly insecure. And the insecurity leads you to be crazy about your bits. There's a theater joke about an actor paging through his script saying, "Bullshit, bullshit, bullshit, MY LINE, bullshit, bullshit, bullshit, MY LINE." Problem is, it's not a joke. Sometimes all you see is what *you* are doing. But that's a pitfall, big time. I don't like to think that way, and I know plenty of actors who don't work that way. So in the end, Stro is very smart to keep the info to herself. It tends to keep the energy in the room from getting too crazy. She's been filling us in on a "need to know" basis. So I have to deal with the fact that right now I am Dancer Boy Number Two. All I can do is show up and do my best. I'm just worried that I am going to be overlooked and frustrated. There go those insecurities I was mentioning. By the way, when did I start calling her "Stro"?

Cast List

Here is a rundown of everyone in the cast. Nathan Lane and Matthew Broderick will be playing the lead roles of Max Bialystock and Leo Bloom, respectively. Gary Beach will be playing the untalented and flamboyantly gay director, Roger DeBris. Roger Bart will be playing his "common-law assistant," Carmen Ghia. Cady Huffman will be playing the Swedish blond bombshell secretary, Ulla. Ron Orbach will be playing Franz Liebkind, the playwright of *Springtime for Hitler*. As it stands now, the ensemble consists of the character men — Ray Wills, Peter Marinos, and Eric Gunhus; the character women — Madeleine Doherty, Jennifer Smith, and Kathy Fitzgerald; the dancer boys — Abe Sylvia, Matt Loehr, Robert Fowler, and yours truly; and the showgirls — Angie Schworer, Naomi Kakuk, Ida Gilliams, Tracy Terstriep, Bryn Dowling, and Kimberly Hester. The swings (offstage understudies) are Brad Musgrove (dance captain), Brad Oscar, Jamie LaVerdiere, Christina Marie Norrup (dance captain), and Adrienne Gibbons. Our stage management staff consists of Steve Zweigbaum (associate director and production stage manager), Ira Mont (stage manager), and Casey Eileen Rafter (assistant stage manager). The music department consists of Glen Kelly (musical arrangements and supervision), Patrick Brady (musical direction and vocal arrangements), and Doug Besterman (orchestrations). Mind you, these are only the people we see in the rehearsal hall. There are countless others we don't deal with — all pieces of the show's whole.

SATAN ENTERS MY BODY

WEDNESDAY, DECEMBER 6:

The week is flying by. My body is medium sore. Not as bad as I thought it was going to be. We learned the Russian Dance today.

Hello? Did anyone mention Russian splits and double tours when we were auditioning? Not a good day for me. When I learned that we had to do those moves (which I can't do very well) I got embarrassed and defensive. Especially attempting a double tour, where you jump in the air and spin around twice before landing. Oh and you have to make it look like you're a dancer too. Felt like a fool. I want to do well but I haven't done shit like this since I was twenty-one. What am I saying? I've never been able to do a double tour in my life. Melissa said she would help me. She's got it all planned out. Have I mentioned that I love her? She's going to come on my lunch breaks and teach me tours. The Russians I just have to stretch into.

There's a moment where we all go crazy in Nathan's first song. They call it the "Nutty Russian" section. During rehearsal, Stro asks the four dancer boys if we had any Russian tricks that we can do. That's when Satan inhabits my body and decides that I would demonstrate some traveling Russian squat kicks. These are accomplished by squatting down and kicking each leg out in front of you, one at a time. Susan is clearly pleased. Satan then leaves my body and I think to myself, "Are you fucking *crazy*????" Eight shows a week you're going to do that? I try to distract her from the squat kicks by showing her some nice barrel roll turns. She nods and says, "Okay. That's good." I can tell that she likes the squat kicks better. Shit.

THURSDAY, DECEMBER 7:

Today we worked music for a number that I am *proud* to be a part of. It's called "Keep It Gay." Roger DeBris and Carmen sing it to Max and Leo to show them what's wrong with theater today. Roger introduces his "design team," who all live in his apartment. Patrick tells us that the concept is based on a famous theater personality, but won't tell us who it is. We have our guesses. I will be playing "Bryan the Set Designer." I have a bit of a solo and then sing a small duet with Ray, who will be playing "Kevin the Costume Designer." Peter enters as "Scott the Choreographer," and Kathy is "Shirley Markowitz," the butch lighting designer. She sings everything down the octave. I cannot wait to put this on its feet. The song is hysterical and cheesy and schmaltzy. Ray and I go into, totally randomly, a bit of the women's duet from *Lakme*. We can hardly get through the number without crying hysterically from laughter. I start to imagine what we will look like.

Interesting development here. I have been given a specialty. My remarks about the "lines being drawn" go out the window now. I am no longer Dancer Boy Number Two. Hmm.

The FDR Chronicles — Only the Beginning

Inside of "Springtime" is a section called "Challenge Tap." Hitler has a dance-off with Stalin, Churchill, and FDR. The structure is as follows: Ulla (Cady) comes out and sings, "Clear the stage for a challenge tap!" From what they tell us, a drop will come in representing flags from the three Allied powers (Russia, Great Britain, and the USA) behind Hitler and Eva as they do a little tap duet. They learned the choreography today. It looks cute and fun, and Cady and Gary look like they'll be great with it. Gary's having a little bit of a hard time remembering the series, but it's just a matter of going over it. Then Ray comes out as Stalin. He does a little scuff step to that familiar Russian boatman tune I don't know the name of, but when you hear it, all you can think of are Russian boatmen. Hitler then comes at Stalin with a tap barrage, sweeping him off the stage. Across the stage, Peter enters as Churchill. The same formula: Churchill does a lame step;

Hitler beats him offstage with crazy taps. Then, I roll out onstage in a wheelchair as FDR. Again, I have been given a specialty. Ahh, the lovely taste of eating your own words.

This is what I will call Old Lady 101. We're working on "Little Old Lady Land" today, which is a spoof on *Follies* "Loveland." I got to rehearsal today and was handed a walker. That's right, a *walker*. By the end of today I was dancing with it. Now mind you, I love props. Especially making rhythms with them and twirling them around. Stro and Warren had us pounding out rhythms and doing butterfly kicks and all kinds of crazy stuff. It was truly like a dance class. They'd teach us a step or a tap rhythm, and we had to repeat it. Then we'd go across the floor or prance about the room. It must have looked hysterical. I thought Kathy Fitzgerald was going to have a fit. She and I have become close (read: we tease the shit out of each other). At every turn today she seemed more crazed. She had no idea that she was going to have to do this kind of stuff. The big point of conflict seems to be the butterfly kicks. They require you to put all your weight on the walker and kick your legs one at a time quickly behind you in an arc. I have no idea where they got the name butterfly kicks. Once you get the weight distribution and warm up they are pretty easily done. But in this case they are a bit dangerous due to our proximity to one another. Stro wants a big oval onstage, with all of us facing inward doing the butterfly kicks. I'm on the stage right curve, and I kept looking at the tape marks on the ground that delineate where the tabs are. (Tabs are thin pieces of "wall" that separate the offstage area into various entrances.) Both Kathy and I were kicking right through what will eventually be a tab on stage right. I told Warren and we tried to fix it, but it's something that we'll have to take care of in tech rehearsals. Kathy and Ray bond through their misery and playfully joke about calling their agents. But at the end of all of it there's that same sentence: "It's for Stro." Ray has worked with her before (on *Big*). Kathy has not. But it doesn't seem to matter. Whatever she asks you to do, you just smile and say yes. I don't know why. Because she's pretty? That would be shallow. Because she's talented? Yes. Because you trust her? *Absolutely*. That is something hard to find in this business. So often you take a job on blind as an — ahem — violinist, and you stay that way, hoping that what you're doing is funny or good or theatrical. With Stro you get this feeling that it is going to be. That she will make it so. And if it isn't she will see that and know how to fix it. Back to "Little Old Lady Land." By the end of the day it was clear we all had some homework to do. But it's going to be so cool when we're all in old lady gear, tap dancing with walkers. That much we can feel.

Stro said the greatest thing to me today. It was at the beginning of the day. I went to give her a "hello" hug and she said, "I wanted to tell you how great I thought you were in *Cats*. I was at the closing night. You really did a wonderful job." She caught me completely off guard. I thanked her, spoke about Harry Groener for a second (the *Crazy for You* connection), then went back to warming up. But after her comments I was already pretty warm and fuzzy.

END OF THE FIRST WEEK

SATURDAY, DECEMBER 9:

It's the end of week one and we've done most of the full ensemble stuff. We sort out more of "Little Old Lady Land." All we have to do is get Nathan in there. Gary Beach came in early to work "Springtime" with us. He's fantastic. There is a moment at the end of the number when cast members get hooked up into what are being called "Nazi puppets." From what they tell us, the performers will kick their legs and the puppets will do the same. (Right now, they are represented by long, 1¼-inch wooden dowels strapped to each actor's back.) So Stro wants to have this huge chorus line of goose-stepping Nazis coming downstage and making a swastika. It's such a great idea. The puppets are necessary because we don't have enough cast members to make that and everything else happen. (For example, because of my duties as FDR, I won't be in a puppet. I'm okay with that. It doesn't sound like something I'd enjoy doing.) There will apparently be bunkers that have smoke-shooting cannons, paratroopers, some fake and some real, coming down from the flies, two German tanks en pointe (that's funny) that shoot streamers out of their cannons, and Hitler will climb on top of the world at the end. I tell Robert, "This is going to be hellish to tech."

SIDE NOTE: Tech rehearsals are every actor's bane. Yes, yes, yes, we all know how important they are. The reason we have a problem with them is because the focus is not on us. That's it, plain and simple. The focus is on the lighting and the sets moving properly and getting the costumes right. Everything but us. All actors secretly think, "We don't need all that stuff. I'm doing such a great job up here they'll never be watching that set change." Then we sit out in the house during tech and watch the set change and reality hits. You can't compete with a falling chandelier, I don't care who you are.

As we run "Springtime" for the third time it starts to hit me. From the first day, I got chills singing "Springtime." Mainly because I couldn't believe that I was really in the show. Today, the chills come with the realization of what we are actually doing.

Watching the Nazi chorus line is really spooky. Stage management actually shut the window shades before we ran it. I'm
thinking this is crazy. Are people going to be okay with this? The
chorus line looks scary enough without the puppets. But I have
to remind myself, *that's the point.* It's supposed to be vulgar and
bad and tasteless. It's hard to remember that when you're up there
doing it.

We finish the "King of Broadway" number, which is Nathan's
first in the show. I love it. I can only guess what is in store when
Nathan starts with us. We've only staged the dancing. My Blind
Violinist track is really nice. (A "track" is a nickname for what
each individual actor does in a show. When the swings and under-
studies learn each part, they are called tracks. It compartmental-
izes it and makes it easier to remember.) It's such an honor to be
given the Violinist. Take a look at any Mel Brooks film and there
is usually either a blind guy or a violinist. I get to be both. There's
a section where we do a hora and dance in a big Jewish wedding
circle, and Abe and I lift Nathan (being played by Lisa Shriver
right now, because the principals don't come in till next week),
into a rolling, street cleaner–type garbage can. There's a push
broom on the end that Nathan will use as a scepter. At the end of
"Nutty Russian," Stro wants to get rid of the broom so that
Nathan can have his hands free. I end my little dance to his right
side, so Warren wonders if there's something I can help with. He
offers, "What if Nathan tosses the broom to Jeffry on the last
beat?" I whisper to Shriver, "Throw it in front of me." I ask them
to watch. The music plays, Shriver throws the broom, and it hits
the floor in front of me as I stick my hand out, completely missing
it ('cause I'm blind). I then proceed to "feel around" in the air
with no luck. Everyone laughs. Granted, it doesn't do a great job
of getting rid of the broom but it's funny as hell, so who cares?
Stro says that we will wait to solidify it until Nathan comes in.

The Russian dance has me worried because I know Stro wants it to be impressive and dynamic. I'm a little less than impressive right now, but all I need is time. I'm more worried about the eight shows a week once I *get* the Russian kicks, splits, and tours. I'm still attempting the squat kicks, but I'm not sure how much longer my knees are going to hold out.

FIRST FULL CAST DAY

MONDAY, DECEMBER 11:

Okay. While there are some things in the script that I think need work, I have never laughed so hard at a *read-thru* in my life. I don't know where to start. I think for me the most exciting part of the day is when Mel came up to me and shook my hand and told me, "We've got a lot for you to do. We're very happy we got you. Lots for you to do, Jeffry Denman." He kept calling me by both my names. He was doing that with everyone. He is incredibly charming and funny. He's like your favorite uncle at the family picnic. Matthew was happy to see me. We spoke about the fact that every musical he's done on Broadway I've been in. Okay, okay, so he's only done two. I'm looking forward to watching him work again. I find him fascinating. Still no word on the understudy front. The guy from *60 Minutes* was there, Mike Wallace. Wanted to ask him about the whole big tobacco scandal but thought better of it. They were filming our read-thru. That was weird. This thing better be good, because the eyes of the world are on us.

They are apparently going to be doing a special segment on us when we open, so they'll be filming rehearsals and performances in Chicago and New York. Yeek. Robin Wagner's set looks fun and surprisingly funny. I didn't think a set could be funny. The rest of the songs sound great. Really great. They are good old-fashioned Broadway musical comedy. And the lyrics are hysterical. There are homages to about fifteen different shows. There is a whole "Rose's Turn" (from *Gypsy*) section in Max's 11:00 number that had everybody pissing their pants. Glen Kelly has arranged the songs and has put them perfectly in line with Matthew's voice. He sounds so great. Gary Beach is a hoot as Roger DeBris. I'm such a fan of his. Not sure about Cady Huffman. I've never seen her in anything, so I don't have much to go on. Plus, I don't think her part is as fleshed out as it needs to be. But I'm not going to judge from a read-thru. Roger Bart remembers me from putting the *How to Succeed* tour together. He's very friendly and asks how I've been and all that. Ron Orbach is super nice too. I tell him that I liked him in *Laughter on the 23rd Floor*. It was one of the first plays I saw when I came to the city. We comment on the fact that in that show he portrayed the Mel Brooks character. Not so sure about his first song, "Guten Tag Hop Clop." They (Max, Leo, and Franz) apparently do a Bavarian slap folk dance. Seems a little forced to me. They have to dance in order to get him to sign a contract? We must be in a musical!

There's also a song in the second act called "It's Bad Luck to Say Good Luck on Op'ning Night." This also feels a bit forced. One of those *we have a lot of people changing costumes, so we need a song here* situations. The rest of the songs work well and come out of the show cleanly. This one seems a bit clunky.

The thing that got me most today was Max and Leo's final song. It's called "Till Him." Matthew sang it so softly and understated, I thought I was going to cry. Started laughing instead. The lyrics are perfect. Even though the movie is brilliant, "Till Him" seems to capture the friendship that Max and Leo share for each other a little bit better. The melody delicately bounces up and down and then soars at the bridge, just likes a good song should. "He filled up my empty life. Filled it to the brim." I'm laughing (read: crying). It seems like a perfect ending. I hope it doesn't get cut.

WEEK TWO

We continue working through the show. Astoundingly, we have the Act One musical numbers almost finished. Everybody is working at incredible speed. I love it. This is the way things worked in Buffalo: get it up on its feet so you can start fixing it.

In rehearsal, Mel's great fun. One day, in the midst of our running "Springtime," he enters the room and starts screaming, "NO! NO! NO! You're ruining my masterpiece!" Everyone collapses, laughing. He's so brilliant. He and Tom Meehan are constantly at "the Table" working on funnier ways of saying things and doing things. (The Table is where Tom and Mel sit. Sometimes Nathan and Matthew sit there too. Usually there are production tables in the front of a room. But this one has more power, I think, because Mel is there. And as much as everyone says, "You know, he's just a person like everyone else," he's still the reason we're in this room. So I don't mind my little bit of worship toward him. Keeps me honest.) Gary had been singing the lyric "Heil myself, heil to me, blow the trumpet, boys, I'm smelling victory." You could see that Mel wasn't happy with it. Every time Gary would sing it, Mel would be at the Table wincing and shaking his head. We've all become accustomed to watching for telltale signs from the Table to see how we are doing. They came back with a number of different versions and finally arrived at "Heil myself. Watch my show. I'm the German Ethel Merman, dontcha know?" To which Glen Kelly then added a four-note tribute to "I Had a Dream" from *Gypsy*. It's collaboration at its best, I think.

We finished up most of "Springtime" this week. The "Challenge Tap" section has now been fleshed out a bit. As FDR, I was given two little USA flags. Stro wants me to wave them around as I come in. I asked Laura Koch, the props queen, for a cigarette holder, a cigarette, and some glasses. As always, she got them in a nanosecond.

SIDE NOTE ABOUT LAURA KOCH: I worked with her on *Dream*. She has to be the most anal prop person ever. And I mean that in the best way. I guess a better word might be *detailed*. She will leave no stone unturned to give the actor a full sense of the part's realism. The wheelchair is authentic. The cigarette holder has a thin ivory ring around it. The accountants at Whitehall and Marks have pads that say "Whitehall and Marks" with the address as a header. The counting machine receipts have a whole slew of numbers typed onto them, that's just in the first week. She is the person working on the storm trooper puppets that we hear about and see prototypes of in rehearsal.

FDR, Eleanor, and Scott

As FDR, I have a line, "My friends . . . ," which is interrupted by Hitler kicking the wheelchair offstage. Onstage there will be a track mechanism that takes care of it. Meaning that a thin path, or track, will be cut into the stage, the wheelchair will be connected to it via a "knife," and a mechanism underneath the stage will move the knife and me along. Until we get into the theater, it is Ira Mont crouching behind me and simulating my cross-stage journey who makes this possible. We try it once. Stro looks unsatisfied. I ask if she would like me to do some taps with the flags.

All the other guys have tap challenges, I need one, too. Since I can't stand, I tap the flags on the wheelchair wheel like drum sticks. Cubby O'Brien (the rehearsal drummer) doubles my rhythms so they can be heard. Stro likes it and we try it again. Just then,

> MEL: Jeffry, yell something as you go offstage!
> ME: What would you like, Mel?
> MEL: Not sure.
> (I knew in a minute he'd have something.)
> GLEN KELLY (from behind the piano): What about "Eleanor"?

Everyone laughs and agrees that I should scream "Eleanor!!!!!" So I do. It goes over nicely. We figure out the exact moment and count that I need to yell it, and after a few tries everything looks copacetic. It's a nice button to the section and leads Gary back into his final solo, which leads to the storm trooper/Rockette kick line. All seems to be going well.

On Thursday my "gay hood" was changed. I went from being Bryan the Set Designer to Scott the Choreographer. Peter and I switched roles. I asked Patrick if it was my singing. He said no. Mel thinks Scott should be a really good dancer. He's just a bad *choreographer*. Peter was hysterical, jumping and leaping around (he's not a dancer, per se). Mind you he *can* dance, but he's more a mover than a dancer. I just nodded and agreed when Stro asked me to change over. I don't really think I had a choice. But I can be a funny dancer, so what the hell.

Warren Carlyle is a true gentleman. I have been working with Melissa on my lunch breaks trying to get the logistics of how to accomplish this double tour. I've got a solid single. Warren stays on me, giving me encouragement and help where he thinks I need it. But he never tries to tell me what to do. He lets me figure it out. I love that. Lisa Shriver is Stro's other assistant. She's quieter. Harder to read, but from what I can gather she seems really nice.

Robert Fowler and I had a funny bonding moment. There are many times during rehearsal when Stro will be standing in front of us, deciding who she's going to use for a particular bit. The ensemble just stands there, all thinking the same thing. The other day, I was standing next to Robert during one of those moments. I started to sing softly, "Say my name, say my name . . . ," a pop song by Destiny's Child. Robert laughed. We both knew that's what everybody was thinking. So any time that same situation presented itself, we'd look at each other and mouth the words and start bopping our heads around to the silent groove.

A Road Closed

This sucks. Ava Astaire McKenzie (Fred Astaire's daughter) is a dear friend of mine. She came to Buffalo several years ago to see me perform in the show I've written, *Dancing in the Dark*, which is my homage to Fred Astaire. We hit it off and we've kept in touch ever since. She is doing a tribute to her father at the Palladium in London, inviting all sorts of screen legends and dancers. She has asked me to perform one of the numbers from *Dancing in the Dark*. This is a dream come true for me — or would have been. I asked Stro for a personal day and she refused. I tried to explain what this means to me, but she wasn't hearing it. Friends have told me I should just take the day anyway, be sick or something, but that's not me. I know that the previews in Chicago are important, but all I was asking for was *one day*. It breaks my heart that I will have to tell Ava that I can't go. I keep telling myself that it's for a reason. Hard to see that right now.

UNDERSTUDY ASSIGNMENTS

SATURDAY, DECEMBER 16:

Stro calls a group of us into the next room before lunch break. I have no idea what it's for until I look at who is in the room. Ida, Jamie, the two Brads, Angie, Abe, Ray, and myself. I start thinking understudy assignments. Stro says, "These will be the covers for the roles and specialties in the show." She announces me as a cover for Leo (with Jamie), a cover for Franz (with Brad Oscar), and a cover for the "Springtime" tenor (with Abe). I'm floored. I had been so focused on the Leo Bloom cover I hadn't even thought of anything else. The Franz cover amazes me. I can't believe that they are going to trust me with that without seeing me read or anything. *Now* I start realizing that Stro does "see me." Amazing what it takes, isn't it? Angie is covering Ulla, with Ida. I'm excited for her. She plays the news low key, saying that she'll probably never go on. She's a lot more talented than she gives herself credit for. After announcing the who's who, Stro is adamant about the fact that there are no first and second covers, but we, as actors, know that that's the creators' way of keeping their options open. That way they haven't committed to anyone, so if someone doesn't work out, they can always go to the other without hurting anyone's feelings. I'm really just glad to have the job. I know from experience that the swing — namely, Jamie — is the logical first choice because of what we call the "domino effect." If Matthew goes out and I go on for Matthew, you have to have Brad Musgrove go on for me. If Jamie goes on for Matthew, there's no domino effect. Plus, Jamie is more similar to Matthew in body type and stature, and very honestly, that's why they hired him. He's a cover. I've been there. So I invite Jamie to have lunch with me at the food court. I take the opportunity to tell him that

I don't care who's first cover or who's second. I tell him that anything I learn I will share with him, and he returns the same. He's a great guy. I maintain that swings on Broadway have to be the most versatile and, in some cases, the most talented people in the cast in order to do their jobs well.

WEEK THREE

DECEMBER 18–23:

We started Act Two this week. Here are some highlights.

We stage the Hitler audition scene. I'm playing Donald Dinsmore, who tries to sing "The Little Wooden Boy" but is cut off before he can utter a note. I try to think of ways to make my little window of time funny. I thought of tripping on the way to center stage, fumbling with my music. But nothing good was really hitting me. The intro that Glen is playing isn't long enough for my taste. I want a super-long intro, then I open my mouth and Gary would cut me off. So I ask if it could be longer, and we try it. When we run the scene again, I decide to go in a different direction with Donald. Rather than silly, make this guy intensely serious. A real, professional, good actor. Then when Roger DeBris (Gary) gets rid of him, it underlines the fact that Roger DeBris doesn't know what's good. So during the intro, I prep like I'm going to sing a heartfelt ballad. I open my mouth to start singing and Gary cuts me off. It's okay. No big deal. Matthew tells me he likes it, thinks it's funny. I could tell it wasn't having an impact at the Table. Stro comes over to me and takes me to the piano. She asks if I can *be* a little wooden boy in the intro. I say "sure" and immediately return to 1984 and do some good old "popping" (as in, break dancing) making me look robotic and wooden. She smiles and says, "Let's try that." Glen writes a new little intro, kind of a Pinocchio-type feel of about two counts of eight, and a new Donald Dinsmore has been born.

Everyone is laughing. Especially at the Table.

Matthew and Cady have begun work on their Fred and Ginger moment at the top of Act Two. I've been looking forward to this ever since I heard about it. I don't go in their first day because I don't want to make Matthew nervous. But I want to start learning the dance and hear all the things that Stro had to say about it. I'm left trusting that Warren will relate all of that stuff.

Sometimes, when you are an understudy, there are issues addressed when a number is set that you aren't privy to. Usually it happens when the actors are working with the director/choreographer. Then you, as the understudy, learn the number from an assistant or a dance captain without that, and they wonder why it doesn't look or feel the same as when the other person does it. Usually it's because you don't know those things. Those are the things I like to hear. Then it becomes less about learning dance steps and more about continuing the storyline. But again, I am sure that Warren and Lisa will be on top of all of that.

The number called "It's Bad Luck to Say Good Luck on Op'ning Night" still feels forced to me. I don't know why. It's like someone said, "We need a song here," and they plopped one down. Granted, it's fun and all, with Nathan running around creating these superstitious situations (like putting a ladder in front of the stage door so that actors have to walk under it or throwing a black cat into the theater), but I think it may be cut down the road. I don't see the necessity. It all takes place in front of the Shubert set. I make a cross with Naomi, my original "Op'ning Night" partner as gussied-up audience members, behind a Matthew and Nathan scene. No biggie.

Having the ensemble wait around a rehearsal room while the

director and/or choreographer is working with the leads can create a monster. Especially this group. Sure, we start quiet. Listening intently to all the wonderful new nuggets of business that are being handed out. But eventually we tire of them having to go over it and over it (*we* could've gotten it the first time), and we begin to entertain ourselves. Usually at the expense of professional behavior. Notice that I am not ashamed of this. Nor will I ever be. It is my job as a member of the ensemble to keep my brain fresh and active. I must be at my creative best at all times for the creative team — that's why I fuck around. Now don't get me wrong. I wouldn't want to be mistaken as the instigator of all of this stuff. Sometimes I am, but usually it's Kathy Fitzgerald. We're in the midst of "Little Old Lady Land" rehearsal. Ray, Peter, Kathy, and I exit early to change back into the design team

Design Team. *L. to r., Ray Wills, Peter Marinos, myself, and Kathy Fitzgerald. This was Ray's first outfit. It was changed after the first couple of previews in Chicago.*

for the Act One finale. Right before this is a section called "Bumper Cars," in which we use our walkers as bumper cars and knock each other out of the way. Stro wants us to make angry old lady noises as we do this. Kath and I are right next to each other and we both have to exit stage right. First run, we just knock into each other. Second run, we start bullishly going at it. Third run, we're screaming garbled old lady–speak at each other. By the fourth time through we're smashing our walkers together yelling, "Cocksucker!" at each other, running offstage, and laughing hysterically. Just as Warren looks over, I straighten up and play cool. Warren says sternly, "Kathy . . . quiet please. The number's still going on." There are the troublemakers and there are those who are smart enough not to be labeled as trouble, but who still are. Kathy is the former, I am the latter. Thus whenever there would be noise or goings-on, they'd always look at Kathy. I'm proud of that. I love her dearly. She cracks me up. She's the big sister that I never had. She has a heart as big as New York and she loves life. And she's talented. Anything Stro gives her, she turns into a memorable piece of work. She's grounded and she dives right into whatever character she's doing. I like her bag lady at the top of Act One. I wish she had more to do. She was supposed to do a scene with Nathan and Matthew before they meet Franz on the roof. (She was to be the landlady who says, "All those damn boids" in the movie. But they cut the scene almost the same day that they had staged it.) Now she doesn't have a big scene to sink her teeth into. But what she's made out of what she has makes me think it's not going to be a problem. She compliments me on my work in a way that lets me know that she really is watching. And she does that with everyone. She's what you call good energy. You want her in your cast, even if she's not right for anything. That's hardly the case with this show. Hell, she could probably play Bialystock.

Life in the World of Mel

One aspect of a show that is truer than any other is that the atmosphere is set from the top down. Behavior is dictated by the director and the leads. In this case, the composer/lyricist/authors, too. When we are trying to come up with new bits or jokes, eventually someone will say something that is racial or "politically incorrect." And while half the group cringes, Mel just sits there and loves it. Stro acts as the arbiter of what is too much and what isn't. But the fact that the atmosphere is charged with that affects all of us.

Stro is busy working with the leads in "Bad Luck to Say Good Luck." The rest of us are standing around waiting to be given our stuff. Recipe for screwing around. Stro and the music department are trying to work out the lines in which Matthew and the gang repeat "Never, never, never, never, ever, ever, ever" over and over. The rest of us are playing various roles. Matt and Robert (who is African American) are stagehands, Abe is the ticket taker, Angie is a dresser, and so on and so forth. At one point I see Matt and Robert erupt into laughter. I head over and Matt says, "Wouldn't it be funny if Robert stuck his head out the door while they're all singing 'Never, never, never, never, ever, ever, ever' and said . . ." Then he turns to Robert, who says in a rhythmic "Amos 'n' Andy" kind of way, "Nebbuh, ebbuh?" And we all erupt into laughter.

So now it becomes about trying to let the creative team see this comedic gem we had stumbled upon. After a few more cast members come over to see what we're crying about, it becomes clear that rehearsal needs to stop for a moment. Stro looks over and says with half a smile, "What is so funny?" Which only makes us laugh even more. We egg Robert on to perform it, which doesn't take much egging. The room erupts. Stro kind of blushes and shakes her head as she lets a smile escape. Kimberly Hester (the only other African American in the room) shakes her head and says, "No. Uh-uh," and then lets a laugh creep out.

Now mind you, half the fun of this is the impropriety of it. And we all know this. But it was at this moment that I realized that the most wonderful thing had happened on this project. Racial issues, sensitive subjects, cultural taboos had now become our garden. We had thrown off the shackles of political correctness and started to embrace all of our stereotypes, our insecurities, our hang-ups. Mel Brooks had given us license to make fun of *ourselves*, which is the first step to understanding yourself, I think. It's the most important thing you can learn. How to laugh at yourself. Mel makes fun of himself better than anyone. He can also make fun of you better than anyone. And will.

Clothes Make the Man, Woman, or Wooden Boy

I had my first costume fitting at the end of this week. I trudged through the snow to William's Chelsea studio and found his people buzzing around like bees. Martha and Tom (William's other assistant) took me upstairs and started trying things on me. They let me have quite a bit of input. Costuming is one of my favorite aspects of performing.

When I was about five years old, my brothers were on the little league baseball team. They were two years older than I. Still are. Anyway, I came home after watching one of their practices and said, "Mom, can I play baseball with Bob and Gregg next year?" She asked me, "Oh, you like baseball, Jeffry?" And I answered, "No, I just like their costumes." *Their costumes!* If that statement didn't foreshadow my theatrical future, I don't know what else was going to.

Back to my costume fitting. The Blind Violinist looks great.

Dark sunglasses, shabby pants, vest, and coat. I ask Martha if I can wear a hat. She hands me a black bowler. It's perfect. Tom runs down to get William so he can approve. He comes up.

WILLIAM: Oh look, it's our little Blind Violinist. It's just *fabulous*. Just change the shirt, I don't like the stripes.

And off he goes.

We get to the "Keep It Gay" scene and I can't wait to see what's going to happen. Martha hands me three sets of very purple spandex pants on a hanger. "Which do you like?" I asked. She said, "Just start trying them on and let's see what we have." They were straight from the 1960s. Which Martha says is okay because William wants these guys to dress *ahead* of their time, which is brilliant. So with my purple jazz pants on, we look for a top. There's a deep purple, short-sleeve shirt on a chair. Add that. It's like a second layer of skin. Perfect. I tuck the bottom up to make a midriff. They like it. Then Tom administers the coup de grace. A light lavender, tie-around half-shirt. I don't even know what it's called, and I can't ask Melissa because I'm keeping it a secret. I had changed into black socks for my fitting, and my white socks were sitting on the chair. Martha leaves to get William to see this before we move on. I quickly grab my socks, ball them up, and stuff them down the front of my pants. William comes in with Martha and I turn around.

WILLIAM: Oh my! Oh my! It looks like you're smuggling a grapefruit in your dance belt. It's great, I just love it! Keep it.

And off he goes.

FDR looks pretty standard. William has modeled the look of

the Tap Challengers (Stalin, Churchill, and FDR) after World War II photos from their meeting in Yalta. So I have the cape and the gray suit, yellow tie. Funny thing is, when I'm in the getup, I really resemble FDR. That'll work.

The last costume is for Donald Dinsmore. For this, Martha gives me an old argyle sweater and a pair of fabulous pants. The color scheme they have me in is perfect for it. I'm all in shades of brown. Look very wooden. I tuck the sweater into my pants à la *42nd Street*. I had been wearing prop glasses in rehearsal lately.

> ME: I've been playing with glasses in rehearsal. Is that a possibility?
>
> MARTHA: What kind?
>
> ME: What about some really thick Coke bottles? The ones that make your eyes look huge. I thought of Donald's face as being like that of an owl's.
>
> WILLIAM: Ooo I like it.

So it was written down and my fitting was done.

I am amazed at the speed with which we are getting things done. It mainly has to do with Stro being so together. She and Warren have everything plotted and planned and practically done before we even walk in. It's going to make Chicago a bit easier to handle. We'll be in good shape before we get there, which means that they can concentrate on sets and lights and all the other stuff.

Stro and Nathan worked on "Betrayed" this week. Because of my bit as the prison guard in the beginning of the scene, I got to watch them create the staging for it. Nathan is just a cedar chest full of bits and gags and jokes and one-liners. He flips a switch and out it all comes. All at once he's Jackie Gleason, Zero Mostel, Harvey Korman, Dick Van Dyke, and countless others. Though they are obvious influences, he is his own force. He is made from an old model. He feels very "old school" to me, which I aspire to be myself. I can't say that my generation knows how to do what he does. To work and work until you drop, then get up and do it again, because it's all you know how to do; it's all that makes you happy. It's not about money or your name in lights; it's about doing a good job then and there because it's the right thing to do. It's pride, really. Being proud of the work you do. That's what Nathan seems to embody to me. Yes, he can be worrisome and insecure, but who isn't? He just wants whatever he is doing out there to be something he can be proud of.

Christmastime Is Here

Melissa is a Rockette, so she can't get away for any length of time during the holidays. I've decided to stay in town with her, rather than go home to Buffalo. My parents understand. In a way, it's okay because I am so exhausted from rehearsals. I will be able to relax rather than have to get on a plane and run around for twenty-four hours trying to see everyone, get back on a plane, and start rehearsals again. My mom has made a new tradition of coming to New York before Christmas. She and my Aunt Janet, my mom's best friend, came up on the 16th, saw the Radio City show, which they both had been dying to see, and left on the 18th. It was a great visit. I had a chance to show my mom Marble Collegiate Church, where I sometimes attend. The choir is marvelous there and the church so glorious, which she was very happy to hear and see. She may not be happy with the fact that I attend a church that isn't Catholic, but she seemed happy that I was at least attending. She becomes more open to my spiritual ideas every time we talk about them. She knows this isn't the same world she grew up in. I like the focus to be less on religious ceremony and more on spiritual involvement. She sees the good in that. She just hopes that someday I will find that spiritual involvement in the Catholic Church.

We all laugh over dinner on Sunday night about the last time she was in town. Namely, me prancing around my living room as Hitler singing "I'm Super." It's strange to realize where I am now: in the midst of rehearsals, thanks to that crazy audition. I wonder where I got the balls to do that.

TRYING THINGS OUT

DECEMBER 26–31:

We've started putting the pieces together. It runs pretty nicely for a first crack. I still think the "Guten Tag Hop Clop" needs to be cut down. Everyone can feel it. "Bad Luck to Say Good Luck . . ." is starting to grow on me. It has an energy that it didn't have before. I try to be the first to admit when I'm wrong, so there it is. I worry about Nathan. He looks exhausted. I don't know how he does it, stamina-wise. He just keeps going.

Matthew is doing really well. In *How to Succeed* he had trouble assimilating new choreography quickly. He would get nervous and second-guess himself. He seems to have gained confidence in the dance department since then. Now his movement is natural and brilliant. You can't learn to dance the way he dances. It's purely him. The fun comes when he finally gets comfortable. That's when he gets cocky and starts discovering all the aspects of the movement. It's a great process to watch. Sooner or later he gets too cocky and screws up the choreo. Then he goes back to Warren like a sad puppy and asks him, "What is that again?" Warren smiles and goes back to square one. And the process starts over again.

I haven't decided how I'm going to move as Leo. I've learned the steps, so they're in my body. But I know that I can't just go out there and start dancing up a storm. Leo shouldn't be a trained dancer. I started to play with "dancing down" some of his numbers. I want Leo's abilities as a singer and dancer to grow throughout the show. At the top of the show, in "I Wanna Be a Producer," I think he should be uncomfortable and uneasy. Even though it is a dream sequence when he's with the girls he should still look a bit awkward. He's not a producer yet. Then in Act Two when he does "That Face" with Ulla another step should be taken forward. Now he's in Fred Astaire land. But still a bit awkward. By the cane and hat dance at the end of the show ("Leo and Max"), he should be smooth and cool. This is what I plan on going into my understudy rehearsals with. I hope I'm not too far off base. Most of this stuff will be just for me, anyway.

New Year's Eve

Melissa and I have been planning to go out to a bed-and-breakfast, called the Pillars, we found on the 'net. It's out in New Jersey, of all places. But it's away from the city and the crazies. That's all I care about. We rented a car after my rehearsal and got the hell out of Dodge. It was great. The drive was lovely, sun setting as we followed it. When we arrived, we found a quaint old English house set in a snow-covered town forty-five minutes southwest of Newark. As we drove up, we couldn't help but notice the rainbow flag flying out front. I looked at Melissa and said, "You think they are gay-friendly, or is this a gay B&B?" She said, "We'll find out." The owners, an older gay couple, were friendly and helpful. I thought they were brothers at first because they had the same last name. But we deduced through some of the informational packets in the room that they were indeed partners. We went for a great dinner at what I think was the only restaurant in town. We went to the bar as we waited for our table. There was a group of couples our age and an older gentleman by himself. The bartender kept the older gentleman busy with conversation. As we waited, I played high roller and bought the bar a round of drinks. I had never done that before. Melissa laughed at me. I wished everyone a Happy New Year and toasted. Off we went. At midnight we were enjoying filet mignon and a fabulous Chianti. The restaurant handed out champagne. The whole evening was perfect.

The next morning we went down to breakfast and introduced ourselves to a teaching couple who were avid theatergoers and who promised to come see *The Producers*, possibly in Chicago. There was another couple, two ladies who didn't say much. They seemed nice, just quiet. After breakfast, we got into the car and headed back, reluctantly, to New York. Wish it could've lasted longer.

REALITY SETS IN

TUESDAY, JANUARY 2, 2001:

Whoa. All of a sudden Chicago is less than two weeks away. How did that happen? One minute we were learning "Springtime" taps, now we've only got twelve days left. I get to rehearsal and can feel the shift. Everybody's in high gear now. The big thing ahead is not actually Chicago but the invited run-thru on the 13th. It wasn't definite, but that's when it's going to be if we have one at all. We really need that, in my opinion. Every show does. You have to get some sort of idea. So you invite people you know and they watch your show and tell you it's great so you can go to Chicago with lots of good energy. Then they go tell their friends what they really think. Everyone's been asking me, "When's the invited run, when's the invited run?" I tell them they haven't told us yet.

Donald Dinsmore got changed today. Now I'm doing more of a puppet-on-strings routine, rather than a break-dancing wooden boy. Stro says it was too much like a tin soldier, so she wants to try this. I love it because I can do the puppet on strings thing better than the robot thing. It gets a bigger laugh from the Table, too. So it's a keeper.

Run-thru went pretty well. The "Guten Tag Hop Clop" is killing everyone. Not in a good way. Ron's knees are hurting bad. The glockenspiel section (a moment where Nathan, Matthew, and Ron all pretend to be part of a German clock) doesn't seem to be landing well and the "Allemande" goes on forever. The Guten Tag "tag," which comes after the song, is Death by Musi-

Donald Dinsmore as "the Little Wooden Boy." *Gary Beach and myself with Matt Loehr and Kathy Fitzgerald watching in background.*

cal Theater as far as I'm concerned. I can tell that they are re-thinking it. But it seems that Stro wants to get this stuff in front of an audience before any major changes are made.

MONDAY, JANUARY 8:

On Wednesday we are doing a teaser. We're doing "King of Broadway" and "I Wanna Be a Producer" for press folk. Now it starts. It's the scary moment when you start bringing the world in to see what you've been working on. In another month the show won't be our little secret anymore.

We felt a small bit of this today as Mel and Tom brought in their wives. Tom's wife's name is Carolyn and Mel's wife's name is . . . oh, what was it again? Yes, that's right, Anne Bancroft. The entire room shifted gears when she walked in. You really can't help it. I mean, come on, it's Mrs. Robinson. At the end of the run she told me how much she enjoyed Donald Dinsmore.

WEDNESDAY, JANUARY 10:

The press event went fine — if you don't mind cameras clicking and people filming your crotch as you do your Russian split. Stro has us all wearing basic black. She was very funny when telling us what she wanted us to wear. She said, "Please, no T-shirts that say *Pippin* or any other shows." Someone said, "What about *Music Man*?" which Stro also just directed. She smiled and said, "That's okay."

PRODUCER RUN-THRU

FRIDAY, JANUARY 12:

Well, we thought this was going to be for a couple of our produc-ers. Ends up that it's for a whole lotta people who our producers have brought. They are definitely an anticipatory group. I'm sure that everywhere they look they see the money they've put into this.

Ron Orbach's voice is shaky today. He's hard on it. Worried about that. He's not having much fun either. He mentions his fears to me at a break. I try to help him shrug it off. For such a happy-go-lucky guy he can be very self-deprecating at times. He seems to be his own worst enemy. But that's the problem most actors face. Hell, that's the problem most people face. I think he'll be fine once there's a real audience out there.

Before doing "Keep It Gay," even though we are all wearing black, everyone in the design team (Ray, Peter, Kathy, and myself) tries to alter their look to fit their character. I tighten up my shirt and turn my baseball cap around, Ray throws a little scarf on, and so on. Matt Loehr plays the underappreciated role of "Sabu," the servant boy. When Roger (Gary) decides to do "Springtime for Hitler" he calls for Sabu to bring out champagne. Sabu, from what we've been told, will be in clothing to go along with his name. A turban, sandals, and that's about it. We get to that point in the run-thru and Matt, who had been hiding behind a piece of rehearsal scenery, pops out for his cue wearing nothing but his underwear and a shirt wrapped around his head. Everyone is laughing.

By the end, the producers are excited and happy. That's pretty normal for a producer run-thru. We really can't tell, from their reactions, how this is going to go over. For us, I believe it went well. The only mishaps were things that will go better with time. But people are working at an amazing pace. Taking changes and directions and implementing them immediately. It's easy because the creators know what they want.

INVITED DRESS

Before

This is the big one. The one you lose sleep over. Some people have forgone inviting friends to this. I'm not sure I could do that. I want my friends there. I wish Melissa could be there. She's rehearsing with the Rockettes for President Bush's inauguration. My big worry is newspapers and reporters and gossip spreaders. This is where buzz starts. Do well here and things will be okay for a while. We might be able to get out of town with our show intact. The thing is, the only audience we've had so far is ourselves. Yesterday's was made up of our producers. They're always going to laugh; they've paid for it. They want it to be funny, so it wasn't a real indication of what we have, and everyone knows that. Lots of prayers and good energy for today.

After

Wow. I'm happy to report that it went over well. Knew more people than I had expected, but not enough to make me crazy. Jenn Dumas, my friend and the producer of *Dancing in the Dark*, was there, supportive as always. She thinks it's the funniest thing she's ever seen. My friends Sean Martin Hingston and Jack Hayes showed up, too. They tell me I've lots of nice stuff to do. I'm not sure what they liked the most. They got everything, that's for sure. "Springtime," everyone agrees, is the one number that isn't quite landing. We all feel that it will do better when costumes and sets and lights come. No one's worried. FDR did okay. It's not getting the laugh I expected. I figure that the costume and the sets and the lights will all help, and it will eventually find its funny place.

Whenever we run the "Betrayed" scene with Nathan in jail, he tries different lines to wake up out of his nightmare. Just before it is the scene in which he is led off by the "black Irish" cop, Robert Fowler. Isn't that funny? So he had been saying "Black Irish!" as he woke from the nightmare. When Nathan got to the moment today, he screamed "Invited Dress!!!" Everyone laughed. Someone caught Michael Riedel and found out that he loved every minute of it. Said that it was the biggest hit he's seen in years. All around, everyone seems to think we're in good shape. Seems kind of normal for us. I don't mean that to sound modest either. We knew that this run-thru was nothing. We still have to get all of this on its feet and running somehow. I've never played Chicago. Don't know what kind of town it is, theatrically speaking. But from what I hear, I'm glad we aren't going to Boston.

We have some time after the run-thru to work on our understudy stuff. It's a bit forced but appreciated. Ida learns "Got It, Flaunt It." We have a chance to play around with "Guten Tag Hop Clop." That number is endless. It's nice to be given a bit of attention so that we know that they know we're working on this stuff. I take my understudy stuff very seriously. Always have. In my short career I have had to go on under the strangest circumstances. In *Dream* I played four principals and an ensemble member during one performance. It was the Jeffry Denman show. During *How to Succeed*, I had to go on closing night because one of the principals was in the hospital. Then there's the ever-popular *going on with only days/hours/no rehearsal* that pretty much any swing or understudy has been through. So I've seen it all, baby. The whole *first cover, second cover thing* is what it is, and I'm not going to concern myself with it. I will be ready if and when they need me. So the rehearsal wasn't great for me because Jamie pretty much did all the Leo stuff. And Brad Oscar did all the Franz stuff. In the understudy realm, knowing is everything. If they know you are ready, that's half the battle. But the only way they can know you're ready is if you have the opportunity to show them.

CHICAGO

SUNDAY, JANUARY 14:

Abe, Peter, Robert, Eric, Jamie, Kate (from company management), and myself are staying at the Lenox Suites, a bit to the north of the Cadillac Palace Theatre. Most everyone else is staying at the Allegro, which is literally above the theater. They don't even have to walk outside to get from their rooms to backstage. Why didn't we stay there, you ask? It's a bit cheaper at the Lenox Suites. Plus, I want to see Chicago. Not like a tourist but like a native. Okay, that's not really going to happen, but I like walking home from work. Plus, the rooms are bigger, and they have kitchens with a refrigerator, microwave, and stove/oven. That helps in the expense department big time. Abe told us our walk was only going to be about fifteen minutes give or take. That's perfect. Everyone has told me to dress warm. I tell them, "I'm from Buffalo. It can't get any colder than that."

We arrive without incident and, after sorting out our luggage, bus to the Lenox. The room is great. I actually have a bedroom and a sitting room. The kitchen is fine. No sign of a grocery store yet. That could be a problem.

I unpack and immediately head out to see where we are. Jamie joins me. We manage to find our way across town to the theater. The house is huge. It reminds me a bit of the Kennedy Center in size. As I make my way into the house, I see the huge light bulb sign that comes down at the end of Act One. It says "Bialystock and Bloom present *Springtime for Hitler*, a New Neo-Nazi Musical." Until this point we had only seen the model version of this sign. It's so exciting to see everything life-sized.

I love theaters so much. I love them most when no one's there. Before the show, before the ushers come in. Maybe a stagehand or two lurking about. Ghost light on the stage. Before opening night of every show I do, I sit in the theater before anyone else is there. There is a calm-before-the-storm energy that I like. Could be something I'm creating myself, for myself, but I still enjoy it.

Jamie and I continue walking around getting the lay of the land. Checking out the front-of-the-house placards. Taking a look at our names on the poster. These are the simple joys of being a performer. We run into Ira on our way to the dressing rooms. He "scolds" us saying, "What did I tell you? No one here until Tuesday!" I tell him we aren't hanging around, trying to get in the way. We just want to see where everything is. It makes things go quicker. Plus, every actor lives by the rules of first-come-first-served in terms of dressing room assignments. So when I found our room, I went in.

There are two alleys within our room. Each has about six mirror spaces. They have Abe, Robert, Matt, Brad M., Jamie, Brad O., and myself (seven of us) in one alley and Eric, Peter, and Ray in the other. That lasts for about two seconds. I take down the sign that delineates the "sides" that we are supposed to stay on, gather my stuff, and put it over where they have the "character men." Abe does the same, as does Brad Musgrove. There is no reason why seven of us should be cramped into six spaces and three share the rest when there's room for all of us to spread out. And we might as well enjoy it now. When we get to New York, we're really going to be on top of each other. The thing is, it's not the actor's fault. We go where we're told. It comes from above. I'm not sure who decides, but they do it according to the type of contract you signed. I hate that shit. It divides casts and pisses people off. There's no reason for it either. We are *all* in the ensemble. We are *all* doing bits and parts in this show. Glad I'm here early.

Jamie and I then decide to get the lay of the land, restaurant-wise. We find that there's not much that's close. By close, I mean New York, walk-out-the-door-and-into-your-favorite-restaurant close. Here you have to look a bit. But there's variety. There's even a $3.99 steak special around the corner. Sounds scary, but you know we'll all be there.

MONDAY, JANUARY 15:

I'd phoned my cousin, Tena Roughsedge, to tell her when I'd be in town. This will be the first time we've seen each other in three years. We grew up together. Our birthdays are two days apart. We were inseparable. Until we were separated. Moved away when I was eight. We caught up with each other on our twenty-first birthdays and drank ourselves silly. Now she's living on the outskirts of Chicago with her beautiful daughter, Kayla, and her husband, Todd. Can't wait to see her.

The last time I was in Chicago I was eighteen. The St. Joe's Swing Choir tour. High school. I can't tell if it's changed or not. I don't even remember what Chicago looked like back then. I was more worried about dodging chaperones so I could fool around with my girlfriend. So this will be fun to come back and see it when I can pay more attention. I bought a laptop two weeks ago in preparation for this. Not only do I want to maintain the journal, I also need to focus on *Dancing in the Dark*. Most important, it will give Melissa and me a way to communicate with each other that will be a little cheaper than long-distance phone calls. I asked the hotel desk if I could get a rate on Internet use, and they sounded like they're going to cooperate.

Eric, Abe, and Robert are all trying to figure out what the gym situation is like. They all belong to gyms in New York and want to maintain while they're here. So now who's thinking that he, too, wants to go to a gym? That would be me. During the week, we found a couple of them. Abe joined quickly at a place farther north, in an area he described as being the Chelsea of Chicago. But it's a little expensive. Eric found Gorilla Sports and got a deal. I walked in today. It's right around the corner from the Lenox. They have aerobics and stuff, but the thing I like best is the boxing class. I'm going once we're out of tech rehearsals. I've never boxed before, but it sounds like fun.

A bunch of us hooked up tonight and went to the Cheesecake Factory. We sat around and talked about our auditions for the show. Having Warren there was nice. It's the first time I've ever been in a social setting with him. Everyone wanted to know what the auditioners thought. Warren told me that my Donald O'Connor pratfall got me the job. He told us some behind-the-scenes stuff that we didn't know. Nothing really juicy, though; he's too professional for that.

TUESDAY, JANUARY 16:

Steve and Ira (stage management) take us on a walk-through of the theater: backstage and onstage and all. Then we start from the top of the show figuring out our spacing and such. We have the greatest stagehands at the Palace. On stage left, I met Lester, who sounds exactly like Barry White. Even does an impression of him. His partner in crime is "Bushman." I ask what he wants me to call him and he says, "Bush." They tell us about the history of the Palace. Michaelangelo is another huge stagehand. I call him the Renaissance man. He's a big, head-shaved, WWF wrestler–looking guy who reads poetry and meditates. They're all friendly and professional.

The Dreaded 10 out of 12

THURSDAY, JANUARY 25:

The 10 out of 12. This is hell time. What it means is that they (the producers) can rehearse you ten out of twelve hours. They have a number of these that they can use, too. If a show is in good shape, as we are, there's no problem. If a show is in bad shape and changes are being made and/or numbers are being cut and/or actors are being fired, the 10 out of 12's can be Death by Equity Contract. I don't think we will be near that area. Everything is going smoothly; there is no reason to think that it'll all go to hell now. Stro is too on top of everything for that to happen.

I have my final costume fitting in the lobby. Things look great. The new shades for the Blind Violinist cover a large part of my face, so seeing might be a problem. Scott looks fabulous. (Stro takes a peek in and I show her my "package." She blushes, and then laughs.) And it doesn't matter how many times I do it, it's *still* scary getting dressed up like a Nazi. Part of me is glad it still feels strange. Unfortunately, I know I will get used to it.

Can I just say that Chicago is unbelievably friggin' cold? I mean, come on, I'm from Buffalo. I didn't think it could be worse than that, but Chicago is. I don't know why Buffalo gets the bad rap. It's like Tahiti compared to this. It's amazing that the people here are ever in a good mood. I'd be mugging people for sweaters.

Got a deal through the hotel today for a free membership to the Lakeshore Athletic Center just up the street from us on the way to the theater. It's going to be more convenient. And, it has a pool! I am all about swimming. That's the one thing that I miss living in New York. I just can't see paying huge membership fees for a gym in New York just for a swimming pool.

Costume Tech

SATURDAY, JANUARY 27:

Before rehearsal I stop at the MAC store and pick up some base and eyeliner. The checkout girl asks me if there is anything else I need. I think about it. Hey, what about Scott? He's going to need some eye shadow and rouge and . . . "Yes, actually, I need some

My Blind Violinist look.

lipstick, blush, and eye shadow." Fifteen years in the business and I'm still not used to saying that. So I pick out some stuff, all in shades of purple to match the set and me. I'm a little worried at how excited I am about putting this stuff on.

I'd been concerned with dancing as the Blind Violinist with the shades on. Until today I'd only done it with regular house lights. Today we used the stage lights and it was okay. It's kind of nice because it takes the glare down for me. The costumes look great all together: the bums and the street cleaner and the nuns and the usherettes and the hookers. It's times like this I wish I were a swing again so that I could see what the whole picture looks like. But that feeling goes away very fast.

My Accountant is pretty basic. I wet my hair and comb it down the middle, real geeky-like. Not that I'm under the illusion that anyone will be concentrating on my hair or me. It's more for myself. I like to differentiate. I think again of Randl Ask in *How to Succeed*. In the show, he disappeared into his characters to the point that people never recognized him. I want to do the same.

When I put on Scott's costume, I notice that I need something hair-wise. I go to Hair and ask Paul Huntley, the wig/hair designer, what he'd like. With his lovely British accent, he tells me, "Well, let's see. Carmen [Roger Bart] is putting his up, so we can't do that. I don't know, what were you thinking?" I tell him, "I'll try something and you tell me if you like it." I go back to my dressing room. My hair is still wet from the greased-down Accountant I'd just been. I comb it all forward on the top and back on the sides. Not good. It occurs to me that Scott might like the film *Ben Hur*, so I comb all of my hair forward à la Caesar and curl the front bangs to the right. It looks absolutely ridiculous. Josephine Baker on a bad hair day. I ap-

My Scott look.

ply the MAC makeup, increasing my ridiculousness quota, and Scott is born. I showed Paul and the others in the Hair room, frightening Cindy, Craig, and Heather, the Hair personnel. When I enter for the scene, I get the reaction I wanted. Horror and surprise, then laughter. I am content. My package got high marks as well. I asked Christina Norrup if it reads in the back of the house; she said it *definitely* does.

I don't have much to say about my Old Lady besides the fact that I think I look a bit like Bea Arthur. We're about the same height and have the same delicate features. Speaking of delicate, I have to say, putting on panty hose is a very delicate matter.

My Donald Dinsmore look.

I went through two pairs before successfully getting them up without a rip — sorry . . . a *run*. It's a whole new world, ladies and gentlemen. Still can't wait to see my dad's face when he sees this show. Not to mention Melissa's.

Donald Dinsmore is fun. I comb my hair over à la Hitler, much like I did for my audition. Doug tells me that my glasses are on their way. Apparently, the Coke bottles I asked for are being made. I thought, "Geez, I didn't mean for you to *make* them. I thought they could be bought somewhere." The funniest thing about this scene is that the girls are all dressed as men. It's hysterical. Naomi makes the cutest little Asian boy. Stro has us stand along the edge of the stage like *A Chorus Line*, so she can see the whole picture. Someone is taking pictures of us. Maybe that will be our new ad.

SATURDAY, JANUARY 27:

When we arrive at rehearsal, Stro announces that Ron Orbach is going to have surgery on his knee. He won't be able to do the preview performances here in Chicago. Brad Oscar will be on for him until he comes back. Which they are assuming will be the opening, on the 18th. Whoa. *Whoa.* This is intense. I didn't see this coming. His knee had been hurting but I didn't think it was this bad. Opinions abound. I'm not sure what I would do if I were Ron. It's hard to tell in a situation like this. It's such a personal issue. He has been hurting quite a bit, but to not be here for the first shows? That's when we're going to be trying things and setting them. Hell, that's why Stro wouldn't let me out for *one day*. And I'm not even a principal. Granted, his situation is different, but she must be going crazy. Ron tells me that he'll be in all the time to watch rehearsals so that he stays up to snuff. Good idea, buddy. Mostly people aren't talking about the issue. Part of me thinks it's a denial of sorts. Things start going bad out of town, word gets back to New York, and suddenly you're a "show in trouble." No one wants that, so everyone's shutting their mouths. Still, this is the last thing we need right now. The swings don't even have costumes yet.

SITZPROBE

SUNDAY, JANUARY 30:

The single best day in the process of putting on a Broadway show. Imagine that you have spent the last month and a half singing and dancing to a piano and drums. Then you get to sit down in a fairly small room and hear the songs played by a *full orchestra*. It's the most exciting day, truly. The show comes alive. It *sounds* like a show for the first time. Peter Marinos was crying through most of it, and that's not something I've seen before. It's overwhelming. Have I mentioned how good the orchestrations sound and how good the orchestra is? Mel is beside himself. Ron Orbach is here to sing his stuff. Some people have a problem with that. They feel that if Brad is starting the previews, then he should sing with the orchestra. My feeling is that it's still Ron's role. Brad is the understudy. Brad will have a dress rehearsal with the orchestra. Ron is not feeling particularly confident now. Singing at the Sitzprobe is something that will help lift his spirits. I'm glad they let him.

During a break, I ask Patrick who will be playing the violin solos during "King of Broadway." He introduces me to Carmen, the concertmaster. I ask her if we can get together so that I can watch her technique. I want people to think I'm really playing the violin. She's very nice and said that we could get together before a show someday. Nice Chicago people, in spite of the cold.

MONDAY, JANUARY 29:

Things went *fairly* well. "Springtime" is a disaster, as everyone expected. The problem is that every dresser, every actor, every stagehand has something to do all at the same time. It's the only moment in the show when it's like that. Usually, if the stagehands have stuff to do, the actors and dressers can get out of their way or vice versa. What we end up with is actors crashing into dressers and each other, crew guys slipping on costumes that have been preset, dressers knocking props off tables, lots of screaming and yelling. "Life upon the Wicked Stage." The Bavarian peasant into Tapping Storm Trooper change is a bitch. We all got on stage in some semblance of Nazi uniforms. The problem is, there are all these parts to the uniforms. Belts and boots that are hard to pull on and ties and all kinds of stuff. John, my dresser for the change, is not the most agile person, bless his heart. He's a lovely guy who tends not to move fast. In the midst of this, the crewmen are trying to set my wheelchair in the track for the FDR cross and get the huge tanks down from the flies. (Some large props and set pieces are tied to strong ropes and "flown" above the offstage wings. This area is known as the "flies" or "fly space.") Meanwhile, James, the prop man, is trying to get "streamer-eens" (colorful, exploding streamers that will be in the tank cannons at the end of the number) into the tanks. All of this is happening within a verse and a half of "Springtime." Once we had a chance to run it again, I think John got the message that we needed to bring it up a notch. The quicker we get done, the quicker we're out of the way for everyone else. Like I said, things will get better. Gay, my dresser for the FDR change, is the opposite of John. She was moving faster than me, and that's saying something. I love quick changes in a show. I really do. They become like choreography. You are literally dancing with your

Bavarians after too much coffee. *Clockwise from top l., Robert Fowler, myself, Matt Loehr, Bryn Dowling, Kimberly Hester, Madeleine Doherty, Ray Wills, Jennifer Smith, Kathy Fitzgerald (behind Jennifer), Peter Marinos.*

Springtime tappers. *Foreground l. to r., Robert Fowler, Jennifer Smith, myself, Bryn Dowling, Matt Loehr, Kimberly Hester, Abe Sylvia. Background (on bunkers), Naomi Kakuk, Angie Schworer, Cady Huffman, Eric Gunhus (on floor), Tracy Terstriep, Ida Leigh Curtis.*

dresser. There's a number in *The Gay Divorcee* where Fred Astaire gets dressed while he sings "Looking for a Needle in a Haystack." His butler is there as he dances into all of his clothes. That's what a quick change reminds me of. Because usually there's music playing behind you. I try to do my quick changes to the accents in the music.

SIDE NOTE ON PRACTICAL APPLICATION OF QUICK CHANGES IN REAL LIFE: In high school I was doing a lot of local professional theater. I was doing quick changes before I took my SATs. One day, while my parents were still at work, my girlfriend, Shelly, and I were upstairs in my bedroom in a state of "undress." That's when Dad drove up the driveway. In a matter of seconds, thanks to my quick-change techniques, I was dressed and down the stairs to greet my dad; and he was none the wiser. I should mention that about five years ago my dad confessed knowing what we were up to. He just never said anything.

All of the rest of my changes are okay. I have time to do my makeup for Scott. Did it for the first time today, and it's crazy. I keep the Scott makeup on for my Little Old Lady. (How scary is that?) Everything else I have lots of time for. I can go back to my dressing room for most of the show.

Can I say how different "If You Got It, Flaunt It" was today? Cady came out looking nothing like herself, in her blond Ulla wig and white dress. From the house, she looked eighteen feet tall. Just a mountain of woman, in a really good way. Now I get it. I have to admit, I wasn't really sure that the Ulla stuff was going to go over as well as they thought. Cady was doing a great job, but I didn't think it was landing. Now, with the costume and the wig and all, it's amazing. Shows you the power of imagination and of Stro being able to picture those things when they're not there. Good lesson to learn.

FDR: Slow Is Not Funny

TUESDAY, JANUARY 30:

My bit as FDR has been under intense scrutiny. I can't tell where it's coming from either. Is it Stro or Mel or Tom or Glen? Doesn't really matter. I just wish I could have the chance to do it in front of an audience first, see whether it works or not. There has been a "need" on the part of the creative team, I think, to try to make everything perfect before we even see an audience. I don't know how realistic that is. A show is a living thing. One of the most important components is the audience. We have no idea how they are going to react to this stuff.

The main problem stems from the fact that the wheelchair does not move fast enough. The "tracking device" can only get to a certain speed, then tends to slow down a bit toward the end. Stro isn't happy with the speed. I agree. Slow is not funny when you're supposed to be careening off the stage. So at rehearsal we try the push, free of the track mechanism. I'm a bit nervous. Now there is nothing to keep me going straight. The orchestra pit suddenly looms ominously to my right. Surprisingly, after the push I do go straight but the wheelchair is old and doesn't roll well. I don't even make it offstage. Feels very top-heavy, in my estimation.

MONDAY, JANUARY 31:

Rehearsal starts with some frustrating news. The *Gypsy* moment in the middle of Nathan's second-act tour de force, "Betrayed," has to be taken out. Apparently they asked Arthur Laurents for permission and he wouldn't give it. When Stro makes the announcement today we all boo. Mel adds his own two cents, which I won't print here. We all laugh and agree. So now they have to cut the entire middle section out of "Betrayed." When they try it, it actually makes a clean cut. The number is still a monster. I just wish we could've seen it with an audience. After watching the original version these past few months I firmly believe that Nathan could play "Mama Rose" without a second thought.

There's a new wheelchair today. At first glance it looks a bit too modern but seems like it will roll better. We try the free push again in rehearsal, first thing. It's unpredictable. It sends me far too close to either the stage left tab or the orchestra pit. Not an option. Someone mentions that it could be put back in the track. "Good, let's set that up then," says Stro. About an hour later, we attempt it. It goes very well. I career off like a mother. Everyone seems happy. I'm glad.

FIRST PREVIEW — CHICAGO

THURSDAY, FEBRUARY 1:

Big day, big day. Rehearsal today, then our first preview. I'm so nervous I can't write.

After the Show

Well, what a relief. They loved it. They were roaring before we even got on stage. Granted, it seemed like they were all huge fans of the film. Add to that the excitement of seeing the premiere, and you have a theater full of easy people. That's okay, though. It'll help us get comfy. I know it'll get worse; it always does. Let me go back through the day.

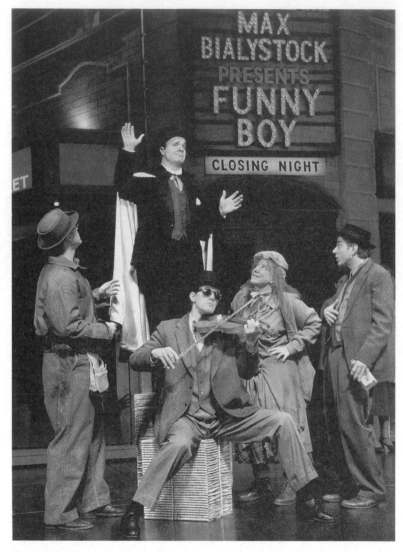

The King of Broadway and his biggest fans. *Nathan Lane with, l. to r., Eric Gunhus, myself, Kathy Fitzgerald, Ray Wills.*

As I walk through the stage door before rehearsal, I notice my old FDR wheelchair on the workbench. Ira comes to me and tells me they have to put it back in the show for some reason. A new wheelchair tonight. I cringe. There is nothing worse than having an unknown entity in a first performance. I ask to go through the moment onstage before the show. They say they aren't sure if they can fit me in. They end up making the time. It goes fine but it doesn't cruise like the other one.

There's a feeling in the cast: "Please don't screw with anything else. Just let us do our rehearsal." Especially considering Brad Oscar's going on for Ron as Franz Liebkind. That's enough of a change. We end up doing some easy dance changes. Nothing major.

Word is going around that Jamie might be on as Carmen Ghia. Apparently Roger Bart's baby was born last night, and he flew to New York after last night's show. It'll be interesting. Jamie seems a bit nervous. But I watch him going through some things during breaks, and he's got it down. He's been on top of everything in rehearsals. No reason to think he won't be able to do it tonight. But Roger arrives at the last minute and does the show.

Everyone is excited and on their game. The costume changes in "Springtime" go fairly well. We're still just making it.

The audience is with us the entire time. They laugh at everything. Later, Stro says that they laughed when the curtain went up and they saw *Funny Boy* on the Shubert marquee. The sound of so many people laughing is kind of scary, like a wave washing over you. But then you love it. I think that of all the scenes, "Keep It Gay" went over best. They were uncontrollable by that point. If this is an indication of what's in store, there is something huge coming to New York. But I think this audience is not going to be typical. I think they were huge Mel Brooks fans who wanted to see the first show. Which is great, but it doesn't give you a representation of what the norm will be. That's fine. It's certainly better than the other way around.

Stro and Mel and the gang come back after the show and congratulate us giving hugs and kisses. It was so nice to have and hear an audience. All our worries about "are we funny?" went away.

In rehearsal I thought I had some nice moments in the show, and tonight it was confirmed. My stuff got great laughs. When I said, "It's good to be the king" as the Violinist, there was applause that stopped the show for a moment. Mind you, I know the applause is for Mel Brooks more than for me, but it felt good anyway. Scott's death-defying swan plunge in "Keep It Gay" got a good chuckle. And Donald did very well too. FDR we're still working on.

Conga! *L. to r., Abe Sylvia (Chief), Robert Fowler (Cop), Kathy Fitzgerald, myself, Peter Marinos, Nathan Lane, Ray Wills, Matt Loehr (Sabu).*

Lessons in Funny Noises

Last night, in "Challenge Tap" there was a laugh when the spot hit me, a laugh when I gave Hitler the "bring it on" hands, and no laugh when I exited. So, according to the comedic rule of threes, we need that last laugh to be the biggest so that it leads to the next sequence. Stro wants to try having me go off the way I came, rather than careening off the opposite side. Stro and Mel are at the production table. Stro addresses everyone through the use of what's called a "God mike," due to the fact that the voice of whoever is using it seems to come from everywhere.

STRO: Jeffry, can you pretend to try and stand up?
ME: Sure.
   I proceed to struggle to my feet as if my legs are paralyzed.
STRO: Good. Now, try and do a dance step and fall backward into the wheelchair.

I smile shamefully, but do as she asks. As I do it a section of cast members in the house shriek with laughter. In my mind, I see United Handicapped Persons Association lawsuits flying my way.

STRO: Jeffry, let's try it again.
MEL: (yelling, sans God mike from the fifteenth row) Don't look behind you, just fall! Hurt yourself if you have to!
ME: Okay, Mel!

Meanwhile, *you* try to fall backward into a free-standing wheelchair, with a tux and cape on, trying to look like you have polio, make it look real, get yourself into the wings far enough so that the rest of the show can happen without your legs dangling stage right, and convince the audience that you're FDR.

I breathed. I did it again. This time, they put the wheelchair in the track so that it wouldn't go anywhere. I saw Mel lean over to Stro and whisper something. Here it comes.

STRO: Jeff, can you make some funny noises as you go off?
ME: What would you like?
MEL: (again yelling) Silly noises, like you're falling!

Ah. *Those* noises. So I do it with noises that I thought might sound like an elderly man falling backward into a wheelchair. I'm not even close. Mel is running down the aisle toward the stage.

MEL: No, no, no! Like this: Ach! Ttthp! Rrrach! Poot!

I don't think any other human being could produce the noises he produced. And it was confirmed when I tried. I had failed the funny test miserably. Mel walks back to the production table, leans over to Stro, and whispers.

STRO: Jeffry, just yell *Shit!*

And that made everyone at the rehearsal laugh.

So we try it during the show. It works well. My biggest worry is the cape. It's so big that it tends to get caught in the wheels and stop the chair from moving. But I manage to keep that from happening. I think we have finally found that third laugh. It wasn't huge but more than before. It'll get better as I get used to the chair.

Melissa Arrives

SATURDAY, FEBRUARY 3:

Melissa arrives today. I'm up early and on my way to the airport. She's going to see the show tonight. I can't wait. Didn't sleep well last night in anticipation. I pick her up at the airport and bring her to the theater. We have dinner with Robert Fowler between shows. She's seeing the show tonight. Afterward, she tells me she loves it. According to her, any complaints I have I should shut up about because we have an incredible show. She loves my bits. Well, maybe not Scott, but the rest of them.

FDR is starting to land better. The laugh is consistent. I love the weekends because the creatives can't change anything: with four shows there's no rehearsal time. I got a note from Warren (on one of his little white index cards we all so look forward to getting) saying that the FDR fall looks too "dancy." Well, now I know I'm comfortable with it.

I called Tena, my Chicago cousin, today. We're meeting next Monday for lunch. I can't wait. It's been too long. She asks me over and over if this is inconvenient, and says that if it is, she'll understand. Tena tends to make allowances for me, thinking that I'm too busy and that everything is more important than she is. I impressed upon her today that I want to spend time with her while I'm in town and we're not waiting until the last week to do it. Tena's dying to meet Melissa.

SUNDAY, FEBRUARY 4:

Both shows went well. The audiences are going nuts. I thought it would die down a bit, but it hasn't. The "Keep It Gay" scene is still the big daddy. The pigeon puppets are getting better laughs than any human, and Nathan stops the show consistently with "Betrayed." At the curtain call, standing ovations every time.

Swam at Lakeshore Athletic between shows. Melissa came with me and worked out a bit. That was fun. We've never done the couple thing at a gym before. I am loving the pool. It gives me a break from the craziness.

After the show the producers (I think Mel, mostly) invite

everyone to a collective birthday party for Cady, Nathan, and Doug Besterman at a new restaurant called Petterino's. It seemed like Chicago's version of Sardi's. They had some faces on the wall. It's right next to the Goodman Theatre. They haven't been open very long. Just days. There's a three-piece band playing. After dinner, Robert and Ida step out onto the dance floor, which starts everyone else dancing. Melissa and I don't get a chance to dance together much so we swing around a bit.

Stro and Warren eventually get out onto the floor, swing dancing like crazy. Probably doing choreography from *Contact.* Just kidding. We're all "getting jiggy" with it when the band starts playing some Latin rhythms. I go over and hang out at the drummer's locale. I notice that he has lots of percussion gadgets: egg shakers, a bongo drum, and some wood blocks. I ask if it'd be okay to play around on the bongo; he says, "Sure." Other people start picking up instruments and playing around as well. Then Stro leads Matthew onto the dance floor. Now it's getting crazy; there are more people dancing than not. Matt Loehr asks the band to play a conga (how appropriate, Sabu), and we start a line snaking through the restaurant, in through the kitchen and out again.

After the craziness dies down Anne (Bancroft) and Mel start to dance. The band starts playing "The Way You Look Tonight," but no one is singing. I go over to the mike and sing it for them. At the end Mel thanks me — "Thank you, Jeffry Denman" — grabs the mike from me, and sings "It Had to Be You" to Anne. They finish with a duet to "Sweet Georgia Brown" (their bit from *To Be or Not to Be*). I turn to the waiter next to me and say, "You don't see this very often, do you?" Everyone in the room knows that we are watching something very special. Melissa's amazed.

Boxing Day

Holy shit. What the hell was I thinking? I have never been so exhausted in my life. News flash: boxers are in fan-fucking-tastic shape!!!!! Yes, I watched *Rocky*, but I guess seeing it really isn't the same as doing it. Imagine that? It was an hour class, and I had my lungs in my hands after twenty minutes. That was before my partner starting *hitting me in the stomach!*

Let me start at the beginning. I walked in and saw a couple of people wrapping their hands with long yellow pieces of cloth. I found some in a bucket and started to do the same, quickly realizing that there is a specific technique. So I got taught and moved on. Feeling very, *very* tough, I grabbed my jump rope and my towel and found a place on the floor. A small, stocky Italian walked in. Tony. He looked like he could and wanted to kick everyone's ass. I found out later that that was when he was in a *good* mood. He put some music on and started yelling in a microphone that made everything he said completely unintelligible. It sounded like, "Cay, cay, cay, lssgo, junnninrowfe, tree mnts." Translation "Okay, okay, okay. Let's go. We're jumping rope for three minutes."

The first half hour played out something like this: jump rope for three minutes, shadow box for three minutes, rest for, like, a second, jump rope again, soft hits on the bag with no gloves, rest for a millisecond, jump rope, put the gloves on, hit the bag, jump rope, give birth, rest for a nanosecond, jump rope, sign last will and testament, *think* about resting, jump rope, watch innards come streaming out your mouth, jump rope, try to spell the word *rest*, strangle instructor with rope. It's good for the heart rate. (Those last couple happened in my dreams during the coma.)

The first half hour was over, and I was ready for more. Here comes the *fun* part. I was breathing for my very life at this point. Tony came over and asked me if I had ever boxed before. I told him no. He said that I was doing well. "Oh, really? I'm doing well?" Well, that only makes me work harder. So we get paired up. I get this big, beefy guy named Mark. Nice guy. Polite. Wouldn't want to box him. Tony gave us a pair of sparring gloves. One guy wears boxing gloves; the other wears sparring gloves, which are basically big flat pads on your hands. You've seen this if you've ever seen a boxer train. We had to take turns hitting the sparring gloves as hard as possible. I went first. Three minutes. Exhausted. Then I switched to the sparring gloves. I figured this is the rest part. Riiiiiiiight. Not at all. If anything, it was harder because the whole time Mark was beating the tar out of my hands. Which took a huge toll on my arms and back. We switched back and forth a couple of times. Then Tony showed us the next level. This is where Guy A punches the bag and Guy B punches Guy A in the stomach with the sparring gloves. At this point, I just started laughing. I thought to myself, "What kind of *Man Show*–taping, Hooters-attending, *Jackass*-watching class have I gotten myself into?" Tony tells me be Guy A first. Oh, goody. So I start punching the bag, and Mark starts beating the shit out of me. Slamming his huge paws into my midsection like I was Mike Tyson's annoying cellmate. I chalk it up to learning how to be a real man and continue. About a minute later, I can't even breathe. Tony runs over and says, "Mark, Mark, take it easy. Not so hard. Jesus, you're gonna kill the guy." Mark says, "Sorry, dude." I stepped back for a moment and said, "It's okay," then watched the years of my childhood and adolescence fly by.

Tony blew his whistle and told us to switch. I smiled broadly. Mark laughed, and then became very serious when I *continued* smiling. But, alas, I treated him with kid gloves, pardon the pun. At least up until the end. When Tony gave us the one-minute warning, I started pounding on him. He was a good sport about it. Took it like a man. Not that I did much damage, but it felt good.

We ended the class with thousands upon thousands of sit-ups. Okay, three sets of twenty, but by then my body was so wrecked, it seemed like thousands. I didn't even care at that point. I just kept moving. Every part of my body ached. Even my sweat was sweating. I came to the awful conclusion that I am severely, aerobically out of shape and that I need to be careful about doing too much in a class like that. Next week's class should be fun.

FDR: No Fall Zone

TUESDAY, FEBRUARY 6:

I get to rehearsal to hear that the wheelchair moment will be again changed. Ugh. Stro assures me that it's not me. We just

Here's the set-up . . . *Gary Beach and myself as Hitler and FDR.*

And the push . . .

have to find the right bit. Apparently, the audiences are uncomfortable with FDR falling. Our audiences are, on average, an older crowd, so I see their point. We go back to me careening offstage in the track. It's still not funny enough. I ask if I can add "Shit!" as I career, and that helps. But I can tell it's still on their minds. To be honest, I feel like the whole thing's going to be cut. It's simpler than we're making it. I just want to do whatever Stro wants. But it doesn't seem like anything is working for her.

Oh, shit!

Uncle Sam's Debut

At rehearsal Stro approaches me and says, "We're going to try something different. Wardrobe has an Uncle Sam outfit that you need to try on." I go down to Wardrobe. Martha tells me that at the production meeting last night Stro asked for an Uncle Sam outfit to be here at rehearsal today. Voilà. This is why Stro is so great. She gets shit done. And not one but two outfits were found in less than twelve hours, overnight, out of town. That's impressive. I have no idea what she wants me to do. But I have a feeling I was going to be tapping now. As I tried the suits on, Lisa Tucci, the assistant wardrobe supervisor, and I agree that one looks better than the other. Only problem is the hat's too big. There's some filler on the inside that makes it sit on top of my head, but if I move around or if someone hits the top, it falls down over my whole head. *That's funny*, I thought. I journey upstairs to shocked looks and "wow's" from everyone. Stro gathers me and Gary to stage right and says, "Just do anything, fill up the music, I just want to see what it looks like." I tell Stro about the hat. I tell Gary to hit me on the head. I do a little improvised tap step, he hits me on the head, the hat falls down to my shoulders, and I struggle offstage waving my arms around. Stro smiles broadly. She calls Mel over. He watches it, he likes it. Apparently their idea was to have Hitler shoot me. Whoa.

Now Stro wants to figure out the tap choreography. We go over to stage left while Warren works with the ensemble. This was the best part of the day. I improvise some steps for her. She watches me like a hawk. For about ten minutes I work with her, one on one, on a twenty-four-count phrase. A Fierce Moment. She connects two steps of mine with a quick, fast-footed step, I end with the hat hit, and suddenly, Uncle Sam is living and dancing. We try it with Gary a number of times, and it seems like a real winner. "It's in tonight," Stro says. And suddenly I get nervous. *Good* nervous. Yee haw! This is what being out of town is about!

I think the most bizarre part of this Uncle Sam thing is the fact that, because of a quick-change, I will be wearing a Nazi storm trooper uniform underneath my Uncle Sam red, white, and blue.

As FDR in the wheelchair, I was used to getting a big laugh when the audience saw me. Tonight when the spot hits me as Uncle Sam, there isn't a sound. Not a peep. It's as if the audience collectively went "Huh?" I do the tap dance, rush a bit on the second step, Gary does the hat hit. I can't hear whether or not the final laugh is big because the hat's over my ears. James (propman stage right) helps me off and I run to my next costume change. Christina Norrup told me later that they laughed. I wasn't so sure.

Next night same thing. No audience reaction when I appear. I've figured it out. The audience is waiting for FDR. Or at least a real person. Uncle Sam is a symbolic figure. Stalin, Churchill, FDR. That makes sense. Stalin, Churchill, Uncle Sam . . . not so much. I tell my concerns to Warren, but at this point there are other things to worry about. I'm trying to let it go. Rumors of the "Challenge Tap" section being cut in New York start to surface. That feels crappy. The Uncle Sam bit stays in the show, but I don't know for how long. The swings tell me assuredly that the hat hit is very funny.

So I get to thinking again. What if we combine the hat hit with the recognition of FDR? I could come out as FDR in the wheelchair, stand up like I'm Superman (so that the audience doesn't feel uncomfortable with the whole polio thing), do the tap dance, Hitler hits the hat over my eyes, I fall back into the wheelchair, yell "Shit!" for good measure, and I'm off. Laughs all around. I thought it was a slam-dunk. I tell Warren. He thinks it's a good idea, but with everything else going on, I know he doesn't have the time to address it with Stro. So that night in my dressing room, I tell her the idea. She likes it but I can tell that something else is on her mind.

Uncle Sam Out. FDR Back In

SUNDAY, FEBRUARY 11:

Uncle Sam lasted for all of four performances. I'm back in the FDR suit being kicked offstage by Gary, the original bit. The technical/props team tried its best to get the chair to roll off fast. More rumors of "Challenge Tap" being cut. I'm bummed. There's something here, we just haven't found it yet.

TUESDAY, FEBRUARY 13:

Melissa left today. She stayed at rehearsal, knitting up in the mezzanine, until she had to go. I'm going to miss her. We agreed that there was too much on my mind for me to be able to concentrate fully on her, but she never really expected that either. Plus, she's starting *42nd Street* when she gets back, and she's all jittery about that. This spring will be nice, with both of us opening new shows.

The Voice of FDR?

During rehearsal I make the point to Glen Kelly that the other guys — Stalin and Churchill — sing something before they do their challenge to Hitler. I suggest that the same pattern should go for FDR. We've set the audience up to expect a short lyric, then a dance. On the third one, we don't follow the pattern. Mel likes the idea and writes (to the tune of "America, the Beautiful"), "The U-S-A will win today!" Hitler pushes me off. Not bad. Or so we thought. It doesn't go over big during the performance. Stro cuts it immediately. Nothing has hit the laugh we had when I went over backward and yelled "Shit!"

THURSDAY, FEBRUARY 14:

My mom sent me a care package today. It had a Valentine's Day card, along with a box of heart-shaped sugar cookies that she made. They were still a little warm. I passed them out at rehearsal. I love my mom. Don't worry, I sent flowers to Melissa.

It's become very clear that Ron Orbach will not be with us by opening night. Most are wondering if he will be performing in Chicago at all. Brad Oscar is doing a great job in his stead.

FDR: Fast Is Funny

The props folk manage to rework the old wheelchair so that the roll-off is better. I'm back to yelling, "Shit!" instead of "Eleanor!" It makes a huge difference in the laugh. Gary and I are starting to get the hang of it. We've gotten into a groove, and it seems that we are figuring out timing and everything. The laugh keeps getting bigger each time we do it.

OPENING NIGHT IN CHICAGO

SUNDAY, FEBRUARY 18:

The show was great. Tena and her husband, Todd, loved it. Laughed their asses off. They were amazed by everything. I took them backstage to show them all the goings-on. They loved it. I was sorry they couldn't come to the party, but I would be thankful later on.

After I saw Tena and Todd off, I took a cab with Adrienne

Gibbons and her sister to the party. We get there and can't get in right away it's so packed. When we finally do, we have to wait to check our coats for about a half hour. I'm ready to chew my arm off I'm so hungry. Finally, I get to the bar, grab a Jack and Coke, ask where the food is, and get directed to a room on the far side of the restaurant. Only about 250 people stand between us. I squeeze my way through and finally get into the room. I can't see if there is food because the room itself is packed. Full of people I don't recognize. I mean at all. No designers, no cast, no crew, no orchestra. It's bizarre. Who is this party for? Clearly Chicago money people, or people who know Chicago money people.

Then, the best moment. I look to the far end of the room, where two giant glass French doors separate the room I'm in from another. People are gathered around the doors and are peering in as if at a zoo. I should have known. When I get to the doors, I see what they're staring at. There, in a very comfy room, are Mel and Matthew and Nathan and Stro and the producers quietly sitting and eating. The occasional press person is escorted in, and then escorted out quickly. I leave disgusted.

I wasn't mad at them for being in there. I was mad that there was a "separate room." I have this funny idea that the opening night party is supposed to be for the entire cast. We had to squeeze around people we didn't know and fight for a space to stand to eat our plate of cold food. When I met up with other cast members, most were livid about the situation. We felt that we had been ignored and left out. It was hard to enjoy the rest of the evening after that. I walked home.

MONDAY, FEBRUARY 19:

The day after. I run into Matthew and Roger on the street. Matthew actually apologizes for what happened. He hated it. Didn't know it was going to be that way. Our conversation leads me to believe that our producers were not all that happy with it either, especially after some complaints were logged. My impression is that no one is used to something as big as this. They don't know how to manage such a huge hit. In a way they are learning as they go. I can understand that. I am seeing it a bit differently today. I am not Matthew Broderick and don't have press grabbing at me and all. In the end, I just wanted to celebrate with the cast together. We can do that in New York.

TUESDAY, FEBRUARY 20:

We are putting Ron Orbach into the show today. Should be painless. It's going to be strange, though. It's already our last week. Everyone is thinking of New York. Good that Ron has been able to watch and take in all the new stuff. He wrote a very heartfelt note and pinned it on the callboard, thanking all of us for our support and patience.

After

The show went well. Ron did just fine. I think the laughs will come. Brad had to find them too. That pigeon stuff works like a charm, though. Note to myself when I go on as Franz: stay out of the way of the pigeons.

All the guys joked with Brad Oscar about having to come back to the men's dressing room and slum with us. He's a good egg. It's got to be tough to do all of those performances, get us through the hard time, and then have to go back to being a swing.

Photo Shoot

THURSDAY, FEBRUARY 22:

Set 'em up and knock 'em down. That should be Stro's motto. That's how she approaches life, I think. Even if something gets thrown into the works, Stro just sidesteps it and moves on. Today is the photo shoot and everything has been organized within an inch of its life. Granted, a photo shoot is not brain surgery, but it can be an incredibly boring and energy-sapping experience if you don't have your shit together.

The coolest thing was that she let the swings in on all the ensemble shots. That way they will be in the souvenir booklet too. One of the frustrating things about being a swing is that there are hardly ever any production shots with you in them. So Stro went out of her way to include them. Love, love, love, all you need is love.

Ron Orbach has no voice. He's been in the show only three days, and his voice is shot. I don't know what it is. Since the start of rehearsals he's been very hard on it as Franz. Sometimes nerves or stress will make my voice go. I think his knee is okay, but I'm not positive. Perhaps worrying about it has made him stressed out. That'll affect your voice, big time.

Goodbye FDR, Hello Judy

What's that you say? "But, Jeff, you already opened in Chicago. Why would you still be working on FDR? Isn't it frozen now?" Hardly.

As I get to rehearsal to warm up, I hear Mel at the piano with Tom Meehan and Glen and Patrick. Mel is going through one of his many showbiz stories. Glen is playing along. It sounds like they're doing their own mock cabaret. As I settle into my seat to get a better listen, I hear Mel talking about "the guys, Goebbels, and Himmler." I listen closer. Glen is playing a soft jazzy version of "Springtime." At the end of the monologue, Mel starts singing some new lyrics and then goes into the old lyrics *after* "Challenge Tap." He's not telling an old story, he's playing Roger DeBris.

They're working what's going to fill the void when they cut "Challenge Tap."

Gary learns it in rehearsal. It's hysterical. At least we think so. Gary works like crazy the rest of the day memorizing it because they want it in tonight. There are only three days left in Chicago, and they want to see if it works. The basic premise is that Roger goes fully to that *Judy at the Palace* place. He sits on the edge of the stage, he mouths "I love you" to someone in the audience, and he proceeds to sing a little recitative that sounds like the beginning of the "I Was Born in a Trunk" song from *A Star Is Born*. I have to plead ignorance here. My knowledge of Judy Garland barely goes beyond *Wizard of Oz*. Gary then goes into a monologue about how "Hindenburg was playing the big room and I was playing the lounge." I don't know a lot of pre–World War II history but I get the point and we did laugh. I want desperately for this moment to work and for Gary to be ready. We throw our support behind him and hope for the best.

During the performance, I exit after the tap-dancing storm trooper section, make my boot and hat quick-change, and watch Gary from the wings. He milks the monologue for everything it's worth. He seems to get lost a couple of times, but I can't tell if he's acting like the "later years" Judy or if he's actually lost. Either way it's funny. The audience seems to like it too. But I can't ignore the feeling that the number (and thus, the show) has come to a halt. The monologue is underscored, but its energy is unlike anything we've done in the show. It also breaks the fourth wall for a very long time. As Gary reveals the storm trooper chorus line, everything seems heavier. The audience doesn't explode like they have in the past. Once again, it feels *almost* right.

Chicago will never see FDR again. I am bummed. FDR had become one of my favorite moments. Even after all the changes, I still liked playing him. Mel told me today that the audiences didn't like seeing FDR lose. They didn't mind watching Stalin and Churchill get their butts kicked, but they wanted FDR to beat Hitler. Guess Americans are funny that way.

Matt Loehr's Birthday Party

Okay, I admit that I am not a big party person. I'll have a drink when socializing, but for the most part I'm clean. When Matt told me about the party he was having for his birthday, I got excited because I hadn't gone out much. There's a place across town, the Mashed Potato Club, which plays '80s music and serves all kinds of "fun martinis." They've cancelled our rehearsal for tomorrow, so everyone's feeling like we have a night off.

We get to the Mashed Potato and find the place practically empty. There's a catwalk and lights and fake smoke. The music is great. Abe and Cady are heating up the dance floor. I dance with Naomi and Adrienne a bit. A couple hours later, people are getting a bit sauced. It's turned into a "wanting to blow off steam" event. We're everywhere, dancing and singing and just getting crazy. Some Chicago PR people introduce themselves and start hanging with us. Matthew and Nathan show up. Matthew orders water. A lot of people were concerned — namely Jamie — because his voice has been getting a bit rough. So Matthew takes it easy and hangs out at the bar, surrounded by the girls.

When the club announces it's closing for the night, the PR girls tell us they can get us into the bar next door. So they did, no cover. That's when you're happy to be traveling with Matthew Broderick and Nathan Lane. We go in and hear salsa cranking. The music, not the condiment. At this point I've become the "surrogate husband" to all the married and "taken" ladies. Mind you, I was there only to protect and serve. The ladies want to dance with a guy, but they don't want to dance with a stranger, so they dance with me. I think they feel safe with me. Rightly so. At present, Naomi is in no shape to be on her own, nor Adrienne. They deserved to get tanked after all we had been through. So I act as dance partner.

FRIDAY, FEBRUARY 23:

Naomi comes up to me and asks if she did anything stupid last night. I say, "Absolutely not. You were very well behaved. Me, on the other hand . . ." She laughs for a second and then looks to see if I was laughing. I assure her that the only thing she has to worry about is the headache she's sporting. Adrienne tries to make me think that she wasn't drunk. Riiiiiiiight. She *always* looks like Gumby without the iron.

Brad O. was back on tonight as Franz. I have a feeling that he will be on the rest of the time we're here. After hearing Ron's voice last night, I can't imagine that he'd be ready to do two shows on Saturday. Maybe he'll try for closing night. I feel so bad for Ron. I don't know what's happening to him, but psychologically, if I were in his place, I would be a wreck.

FINAL SHOW IN CHICAGO

SUNDAY, FEBRUARY 25:

We don't have to be back to rehearsal until Wednesday! They're giving us Tuesday off. Two days in a row off before New York? We *must* be in good shape. This is unheard of.

Nathan had some very nice things to say at the end of the curtain call today. He thanked Chicago for being such an open and warm town for us. It was great. I wished that Mel and Stro had been there to make an appearance. I think the audience would have really liked that. They had already left for New York to get a head start. Eric and I have decided to get an earlier flight tomorrow morning. Some folks are trying to get out tonight. I'm going to bite the bullet. If I can get out before our scheduled flight tomorrow afternoon, I'll be happy. I'd have a bit of daylight to enjoy tomorrow.

A bunch of us went out for seafood. I sat next to Ida. It was the first time I had spent time with her. She's great, and I enjoyed her company tonight. I'm exhausted. See you in New York.

HOME AGAIN — NEW YORK

TUESDAY, FEBRUARY 27:

Today, I was running errands all over Midtown. Got some acupuncture, met up with Nancy and Dennis to catch up on what's been happening. I'm making my way up the West Side when I get a call on my cell phone. It's Ira. He tells me Brad Oscar has been offered the part of Franz Liebkind and has accepted. I feign calm and say, "Oh, okay. That's great." Then hang up. All at once, I am happy for Brad and sad for Ron. A Broadway dream and a Broadway nightmare in one stroke.

I run into Brad Musgrove and Abe in front of the 72nd Street subway station and tell them. We all give a small "whoa."

Then I go to the St. James Theatre. It's a mess. Can barely get through the stage door, there's so much crap everywhere. They've started painting dressing rooms so there isn't much in the way of signs pointing to where we will be stationed. I like the feel of the theater, though. I'm an actor, I always do.

Much like the people who inhabit them, theaters are funny. Each show has a different feel, and that feel gives the theater its atmosphere. It's like the difference between walking into K-mart and walking into the Gap. Different feel, yes? I recently visited the Richard Rodgers Theatre to say hello to a friend who's doing *Suessical.* The Rodgers is where we both did *How to Succeed.* But when I walked in, it was like I had never been there before. It felt foreign. Two other shows had been there in the interim, *Footloose* and *Steel Pier.* I find it fascinating that shows have personalities all their own. You couldn't have it any other way. Theater folk are territorial. We want to believe that our show is the only one ever at that theater. We make it so by pushing out the old energy from the previous show. It's serious feng shui. I don't know how we do it, we just do. As I was climbing the stairs at the St. James, I could feel and see remnants of *Swing!* In a week, that will all be gone.

WEDNESDAY, FEBRUARY 28:

At rehearsal this morning we congratulate Brad O. He appears to still be in swing mode. That's okay, he'll get it. When Nathan arrives, he looks at Brad and says, "So . . . what's been going on?"

We went back to Little Old Lady 101 today. Well, that's not true. Now it's more like second- or third-year Little Old Lady. Stro adds some more walker tap choreography. It's all good. They're tiny changes but they make your brain skip a beat when you get to them.

THURSDAY, MARCH 1:

Peter, Ray, Kathy, and I are being interviewed by UPN this morning for a special that they are presenting around the time that we open. As I walk into the rehearsal studio hallway for the interview, I hear someone playing the "Challenge Tap" section. I look at Ray and say, "That's 'Challenge Tap.'" He says, "No. They cut it. It's dead." I listen more. "That's 'Challenge Tap.' I'm sure of it." We go in for the interview.

UPN has been following us around and taking pictures.

Today they want to interview the three Old Ladies and the design team. It's all standard interview stuff. We laugh and have fun. Ray's a party pooper, though. Any time they ask about what happens in the show, he says, "We really shouldn't give that away, you know? Don't want to ruin it." The first two times, it was fine. But even about things that aren't all that important, he keeps saying it. "Sorry, we can't give that away" tends to make for bad interview copy. The rest of us don't follow that form. When this program airs we'll have been on for four weeks already. The reviews will have been written and will come out the next day, and we can't keep much secret after that. In the end, I was just glad to be part of it. I always get nervous being on TV. I hate being worried about the way I look. I've never gotten comfortable with that.

Before I leave rehearsal, I check the schedule for tomorrow: REHEARSAL — GARY BEACH, PETER MARINOS, RAY WILLS, JEFFRY DENMAN, CADY HUFFMAN. All of the people involved in "Challenge Tap." That's when I realize that, by cutting that section, they had cut out Ulla's only solo singing and dancing part in "Springtime." Later in the show, when Matthew reads the reviews in the paper that "A new star was born on Broadway . . . Ulla," it won't make sense to the audience. It seems they are rethinking that so as not to lose the "Ulla factor."

The K.I.S.S. Method

FRIDAY, MARCH 2:

Stro comes over, as she has so many times before, with a smile on her face and her eyes half-apologizing. She starts with a very heavy "Okay," as she always has when she has been trying to sort out new ideas.

STRO: What we're going to try is this. You come out, no lines, no singing, do the tap-dancing flags, Gary pushes you off, done.

It's the K.I.S.S. method: keep it simple, stupid.

ME: (with hope) Do you want me to yell "Shit?"
STRO: (decisively) No. (Then, not so decisively) Not yet. Let me see it without. Who knows? Probably not.

This is probably the only time in the entire process Stro does not have a decisive answer. But FDR was back in the show at least. That makes me happy.

THURSDAY, MARCH 8:

There hasn't been a lot of rehearsing lately. The choreographic changes in Little Old Lady land I really like. We don't get to do the Bumper Car section with the walkers anymore, but she's added more "tapping" moments, which work better. It makes it more of a traditional tap number.

There have been some nips and tucks. Some staging changes for the designers in "Keep It Gay." She's got us on the stairs for more of the number. I'm thinking that it fills the picture out a bit more. They worked on the cop scene as always. I don't know if that will ever feel settled. I think it suffers from the same malady as FDR. Thank God the "Guten Tag Hop Clop" got shortened in Chicago. That scene runs so much better now.

Generally, the energy in the room is relaxed. We are trying to get a feel for what's going on in the city. The lines outside the theater are surprisingly long. Our producers tell us it's been that way since we opened in Chicago. Guess people were watching. We're not complacent, though. Nathan and Matthew talk about the ever-dreaded "backlash." No matter how well a show does there is always a "backlash" that comes. Sometimes from the theater community, sometimes from further out. Usually it happens when a show doesn't live up to its hype. That's what I worry about. We can't control the things people say. We can only go in and do our best. Things can start to get frustrating.

We had to do a run-thru today. This was *very* difficult. We have just spent a month in Chicago, onstage with orchestra, props, costumes, and, most important, an *audience.* Now we do it with a piano and drums, in rehearsal clothes, with rehearsal props for a handful of people who weren't going to laugh because they wrote the jokes. It doesn't get more tiring than that. Nathan wasn't having it. I'm half and half on this one. On the one hand, we haven't run the show in its entirety since we closed in Chicago. That's almost two weeks ago. We have to see how the changes affect the flow. On the other hand, we are now in New York, starting to doubt that we are funny. The last thing we need is a run-thru with no laughs. After the audience has entered the process, it's hard to take them away. They become part of the rhythm. (That's why understudy rehearsals are so painful. For three hours you're working to make people laugh who aren't ever going to laugh because they know what you're doing.) But should any director let his or her actors dictate what he or she decides to do? Well, let me put it this way: the saying about lunatics running the asylum leaps to mind.

THE CAST RECORDING

SUNDAY, MARCH 11:

At the top of my list of "Favorite Moments in Putting on a Broadway Show" is the first Sitzprobe, which we've been through. Next on the list is the cast recording. The Sitzprobe is the first time you hear it. There's nothing more exciting than that. The cast recording is exciting because there comes a moment when you realize that you're putting this down *forever*. I think back to how many shows I put up in Buffalo using Broadway cast recordings. How many stars I listened to for style and character. How many hours I spent in my living room with the doors closed, singing, dancing, even conducting my own one-man performances of *Sweeney Todd, Les Miserables, Jesus Christ Superstar*. How many careers I followed on the backs of LP jackets. Ensemble members from one show who made the jump to principal on another. The cast recording should be a true representation of the show. Besides the Lincoln Center archives and a *Playbill*, it is the only thing that lives beyond the run. I was so bummed that *Dream* never got recorded. It probably would have made a better recording than a show. But it's lost forever. Every show that opens on Broadway deserves to be recorded.

Patrick Brady is on a mission today. He is going to get the recording done in one day if it kills him and everybody in the studio. He keeps everything moving. We'll cut it pretty close. My worry is that the quality is going to suffer. We'll see.

PBS was everywhere. They are shooting a documentary of the making of the cast recording. It's crazy. We're at the point now where if we *don't* see a camera crew behind, in front of, or on top of us whenever we take a walk, we think we're closing.

The studio's like a farm. We're herded in, we sing, we're herded out, we graze out in the green room for a bit, we're herded back in, we sing more, herded out, etc., etc., etc. The problem with the recording studios at the Edison Hotel, where we are, is that they aren't made for a ton of people. When we recorded *How to Succeed*, we did it at the Hit Factory, a spacious recording studio in Hell's Kitchen. Oh, well. You do what you have to.

Toward the end of the day we get to my favorite part: putting down the taps for "Springtime" and the Walker Dance in Old Lady land. We had to dance on a small square of dance floor tiles. The kind they set up for wedding receptions. Very slippery. Microphones are spaced around us; cameramen and -women are hovering as always. Our biggest problem is with the earphones (called "cans"). My cord is a bit short so I have to be careful where I dance. Brad Musgrove's cord got caught on his walker, causing some havoc, but nothing terrible. When the cameras are on, everybody's on their best behavior. Not that we wouldn't be normally, but there's an extra bit of "oomph" there.

I go over to Robert and suggest that he get his "Nebbuh, Ebbuh?" line in somewhere. We jokingly plot a way to get it in. I hate to say it, but it is the one company joke that still gets us all laughing. I think it's because of Robert. He would never offend anyone. So when he does it, it has an innocence that is priceless.

Part of the fun of today was watching everyone jockeying for position so as to have good camera time. I can't say that I wasn't thinking about it too. But I got to a point where I just had to let it go. If I'm on it, I'm on it. It's not like some film director is going to look at this documentary and go "Oh my God! Him! I need *him*! That's my Hamlet!" When I start to get like that I just look over at Robert, watch his demeanor, and try to follow suit.

At one point between takes of "Keep It Gay," the cameras roll over to catch Nathan, Matthew, Robert, Matt, and me in conversation. Nathan notices the cameras and says to Matthew, "I think it's time for an interview with Mr. Brando." Matthew does the funniest impression of Marlon Brando I've ever seen. He shies away at first, then can't resist. Nathan proceeds to ask "Mr. Brando" questions about the recording and what he thinks of it. When "Mr. Brando" starts answering, we are on the floor. Toward the end, Matthew realizes that the cameras are capturing every nuance and lisp that he's doing. He mentions something about national television and stops the "interview." Much to our relief. Our diaphragms are in spasm. Thank God it's at the end of the day. I'm in no shape to sing after all that. I hope the footage makes it into the final cut.

Start Tech

Crazy. There is no room. The third scene in the show takes place at Leo Bloom's place of employment, Whitehall & Marks. On-stage, this is represented by a long, narrow palette that is set into a track on the floor, which rolls on and off. When we go off, the palette splits and bends around the corners of the backstage area. We face up against the fly lines on stage right with not an inch to spare. At the end of Act One before the finale, we have to climb through set pieces to get to our costume changes. As you do your changes you are dodging stagehands and dressers and Hair people. Doing more choreography than is onstage. But as much as the space issue keeps stopping us, we got pretty far into Act One today. Everyone's doing the best they can. The stagehands deserve major kudos.

All the stagehands are named Bob. Just kidding. There are actually only three Bobs. But get this: stage right, the two deck guys are Bernie and Bob; stage left, Barnie and Bob. What are the odds? Easy to remember. There's also Eddie and Timmy Mac. They sound like the guys who will be running the softball team this summer for the Broadway show league. There's Tom, a Rich, and a Richie, who generally look busy. (I'm not clear on jobs yet, but I'm trying.) There's James, who pages the curtain for me a couple of times. They're all nice. And they've all heard how good the show is. That's another thing: if you want to know if a show is going to run, ask the stagehands. Nine times out of ten, they know first. It's hardly *ever* the actors. We're the last to know. But the Bobs and Barnies and Richies and Bernies are all saying stuff like, "So we hear you guys are pretty funny, huh?" Apparently they have connections to the guys in Chicago.

DRESS RUN

SATURDAY, MARCH 17:

It's great to be back into costume. However, our intermission was ninety minutes long due to the lack of room backstage. Bernie tells me they'll be lucky to get it down to forty-five minutes. Never anything less than that. The main issue is that we have to have two huge office sets because of Ulla's joke in the second act where she paints Max's office white. Add that to the Roger DeBris set, the "Springtime" stairs and bunkers, and the courtroom set, and you have too much set and not enough theater. Bernie thinks they could get it down with another stagehand. But I'm sure the producers are concerned with that. It will be interesting to see how this pans out. Can't have a forty-five-minute intermission. Hell, you get criticized for having a *twenty-minute* intermission.

The Producers of Over-ness

TUESDAY, MARCH 20:

A gypsy run is your final dress. It's called that because you invite all the "Broadway gypsies" to come watch. I don't know why Broadway performers are called gypsies. It probably has to do with the fact that we move from show to show, much like real gypsies move from place to place. Gypsy runs are usually raw and full of nervous energy.

The intermission runs twenty-seven minutes. It's amazing how they've cut it down. The extra man they hired helps big time. When you have to spend the money, you have to spend the money. (It's amazing how quickly things like that get taken care of when the show is a hit.) Watching what happens during the intermission is crazy. Should sell tickets to that. I don't envy any of the stagehands.

Noah Racey, Dennis Stowe, Dan Acquisto, and Jon Erik Parker are my guests today. During the show, when I come out as Scott, I hear Dennis screaming/laughing. I haven't told anyone what I do in the show, so that they'll be surprised. When we meet after the show, Dennis is practically in tears. Partly because he had been laughing so much, and partly because he's proud of me. Noah loved it, as did Dan and Jon Erik. Good marks all around. And I know I can trust these guys. Jon Erik says, "I have nothing to say. You're *over* [pronounced "ovah"]. You are over-ness. It should be called *The Producers of Over-ness*." I can't put it much better than that.

FIRST PREVIEW — NEW YORK

WEDNESDAY, MARCH 21:

My agent, Ann, and her husband, Gene Jones, were in the audience tonight. After the show, which went great, we met briefly. Gene says it's the funniest thing he's seen since the original *Forum*. That's impressive. They both think that we will walk away with all of the Tony awards. Nice thought, but the Tonys are a long way off. A lot can happen between now and then.

Melissa gave me a "first preview" gift tonight. She found a miniature violin and violin case. Complete with bow and strings. It's just beautiful. She does gifts good.

Nathan was incredible tonight. I stood offstage and watched him pour even more on, which I didn't think was possible. The audience feeds him. That's why he gets angry when they don't respond.

Tonight's intermission ran about twenty minutes. Everyone seems to think all will be okay.

K.I.S.S. FDR

The quick and short FDR moment works fine. It's not as big a laugh as we'd had, at times, in Chicago, but I think everyone knows that we had to cut our losses. I continue to try to find the funny in the moment. FDR is back, and all's right with the world. Mel approaches me:

ME: So "Shit" is definitely out, huh?

MEL: Yeah. It was cheap. Either I have to come up with a better exit line, or there's going to be none at all. I can't always rely on cheap stuff for laughs.

I will always remember him saying that. (This from the man who etched in my head the image of cowboys farting around a campfire.) It exemplifies Mel's struggle during this process. He desperately wants Broadway to take him seriously. I think because he respects theater so much. It's where he comes from, really. It was his first love. He has conquered every other medium of entertainment. This will be the grand slam.

Late Show with David Letterman

TUESDAY, MARCH 27:

We performed on *Letterman* today. It airs tonight. It looked great. This is the first time any of us have been able to see what we look like in the show. Letterman is notorious for keeping the Ed Sullivan Theatre freezing cold. I was glad I had my coat and vest and hat. Could practically see my breath. I'm not kidding. Letterman doesn't let many musicals do numbers but he really likes Nathan and you can tell. Nathan had an interview, which was pretty funny. Then, after a commercial break, we did "King of Broadway." We had to scale it down a bit due to spatial concerns. The audience liked it.

OPENING NIGHT

THURSDAY, APRIL 19:

Before

Well, my parents got in okay. They're on their way from the airport right now. I have some major running around to do today. I picked up miniature violins, like the one Melissa gave me, as opening night gifts for Stro, Tom Meehan, and Mel. I had the cases engraved and have to pick them up today. I need to finish up my gifts for the masses. I did my traditional Looney Tunes rendering of the show. It started back in *How to Succeed* when Jerome Vivona noticed that the characters in our show paralleled Looney Tunes characters (Bugs, Daffy, et al.). That got me thinking: What if there was a cartoon of *How to Succeed*? Who would play who? So I started drawing some ideas and showed them to Jerome. We ended up collaborating on "Looney Tunes Presents. . . ." I have since done three more. One for *A Foggy Day*, which I did up at the Shaw Festival, one for *If Love Were All*, and one for *Cats*. My favorite part of presenting them is how amazed people are when they see how the characters parallel. I think it has to do with the universality of the cartoon characters. For example, in my *How to Succeed*, Bugs played Finch, Daffy played Bud Frump (Finch's nemesis). You think through *The Producers* and you have Yosemite Sam playing Max Bialystock, Bugs playing Bloom, with Daffy playing Roger DeBris. The Looney Tunes characters are so well developed that they can be very versatile. I love it. I usually have everyone sign the thing and hang it on my wall. I'm giving smaller renditions of the drawing as gifts. I'll have them sign it later. I don't want to give away the surprise.

The best part of opening night is walking into your dressing room before the show. Opening nights are usually scheduled for 6:30, so I like to get to the theater early to hand out my gifts and see what I've gotten myself. It's better than Christmas. Well, not spiritually, just in the greedy, gift-getting sense. Blue Tiffany bags stand majestically on the chairs, on the dressing room tables, and even all over the floor. Then you see the flowers and all the other goodies that have been carried to your room. Cady and Angie gave, to each dressing room, a bucket of beer, complete with ice, for after the show. Matthew and Nathan gave everyone a producers' hat key ring from Tiffany. Stro gave us champagne flutes from Tiffany, gorgeous. Mel gave a small producers' hat charm with a lovely card. I'll stop there or else it'll sound like a wedding thank-you list. In short, the gifts were great, and people loved my drawing.

The Show and Party

What a great evening! I'm wasted. I'd never been to Roseland before. I guess if you're going to go, the way we went tonight is the way to do it. Opening nights that I've been involved in have been moderately big things. A bit of press, a bit of a crowd. This was far beyond anything I had experienced before. I had to step outside of it a couple of times.

Surprisingly, the show was a bit anticlimactic. Number one, we had such a great audience for our final preview, it was going to be hard to match that. But you'd think that "opening night" would be more exciting for the audience than "the night before opening night," wouldn't you? Number two, I was holding the closing of *Cats* up as a barometer. In a way, I was hoping that our evening wouldn't come close. I didn't want anything to eclipse that memory so quickly. I had a feeling that it was going to be a losing battle. (I was wrong. The closing of *Cats* is still at the top of my list as the loudest and most supportive crowd I've ever been in front of.) Number three, the orchestra section of the theater was filled with "famous" people. Larry King, Mary Tyler Moore, Michael J. Fox, Alec Baldwin, Eric McCormick, Demi Moore, Glenn Close, John Waters, Lauren Hutton, Barbara Walters, just to name a few. But if they found the show funny, they weren't

Mom, me, Melissa, and Dad.

showing it. They seemed to be watching to see if everyone else was laughing, not wanting to let their guard down in front of their Hollywood pals. It was frustrating for us, especially considering the fact that we could hear our friends and families up in the mezzanine hooting and hollering and having a ball. *They* were letting themselves enjoy it. It was strange: we could hear laughs, but they seemed to be coming from far away. Funny thing is, at the party, where every big star was interviewed, they all said how they couldn't stop laughing. I wanted to say, *"But we saw you! We were looking right at you! You didn't laugh once!"*

All the jokes went over. There were no mishaps. Word was that some of the reviews had been "previewed" and that things looked very good. But after being involved with *Dream*, I don't trust it till I see it in print. Everyone from my agent to a stranger at the bank has told me that this is going to be the biggest thing ever. I still don't believe it. I wonder if an actor can ever fully do that?

At the party I'm reading the reviews just like they do in old movie musicals. They are unqualified raves. All around. I didn't read a bad word anywhere. It's starting to sink in. My parents and Melissa look at me like, "Are you crazy? Of course they're raves!"

I finally see an opportunity to give Mel his violin. I had found Stro at the theater, grabbed Tom Meehan as we were entering the party, but, as you can imagine, Mel was swamped everywhere he went. So the party dies down a bit and the four of us stroll over to his table.

As I approach, I notice Michael Riedel standing behind Mel, probably goosing him for info. I introduce myself again. He remembers me from *Cats's* closing night. It's a crazy, kooky universe. There I had been at the closing, talking to him about whether or not this was going to be a hit. I want so desperately to remind him of what he had said, but I thought better of it. He was such an immediate and huge supporter of the show right from the get-go, I can't fault him.

I continue waiting in the Mel Brooks line. We squeeze around, and I grab his attention. The look on my dad's face is priceless as I introduce him. As I give him the violin, my mom snaps a picture. Her camera has one of those anti–red eye "I'm going to flash one thousand times before I actually go off" cameras. I think Mel thought he was having a stroke. I introduce them to Anne Bancroft. She's lovely, as always, and has complimentary things to say, as does Mel. We make our way out of the craziness and decide to go home. My parents are clearly exhausted; I'm glad they're staying for another day.

WEDNESDAY, APRIL 25:

When I was in high school in Buffalo, I became friends and worked for the vice principal, Brother Fred Dihlmann. In Fred I found a man who was incredibly devoted to his faith and incredibly devoted to musical theater. In the years since, he has always been there for me, watching and encouraging me as I follow my dreams. He came to see the show today. He loved it. I was a bit worried because of some of the "blue" material, but he loved it. I went next door to have dinner with him and his guests. Just as I love showing my parents what I have been able to achieve, I feel the same way about Fred.

Oklahoma!

FRIDAY, APRIL 27:

I have an audition today. Yes, I know I just opened a show a week ago. So what am I doing auditioning? Well, this show doesn't start rehearsals until December 2001. It's for Trevor Nunn and

Stro's revival of *Oklahoma!* Tara is calling me in for Will Parker. I picked up the sides and the music yesterday and have everything memorized. They also want a monologue. Gene offered one that he thinks is appropriate.

I get to Chelsea studios and wait outside. My worlds are crashing together. Trevor saw me as Munk at the closing of *Cats.* Stro I don't even need to talk about. I'm hoping this all bodes well for me. This is my opportunity. A principal in a high-profile show.

I go in. Trevor greets me with a firm handshake.

TREVOR: Well, this will be the third time I'll have seen your work.

ME: The third?

TREVOR: I saw the final performance of *Cats* and I caught last night's performance of *The Producers.* Very nice work.

I'm agog. We talk about *Cats* a bit. Then he asks what I've prepared for my monologue. I tell him it's Bo Decker from *Bus Stop.* He commends me on my choice. (*Thank you, Gene.*) I go into the monologue and it goes great. I nail everything. He's pleased. I sing "Kansas City" and he ponders a moment. He crosses over to me, grabs my arm, and starts whispering to me.

TREVOR: Will has just come in from Kansas City, yes? Alright. For us, that's like you coming back from Mars and retelling all of the incredible things you've seen. Things that are inexplicable. A horseless carriage, a skyscraper, a telephone, these are all things that Will's friends can't even comprehend. So he becomes the conduit. And some of these things scare you, because you can't explain them either. Try it again.

I totally get what he wants. I attempt to give it to him. Afterward he smiles and says, "Well done. Truly, well done. Thank you so very much." As she walks me out, Tara tells me to stick around.

When she comes out again, she asks if I can come on Monday for a callback. I say of course. She gives me more music and sides to learn. She tells me I will be reading the Will/Ado Annie scenes with Jessica Boevers.

MONDAY, APRIL 30:

At the callback, Trevor starts by having me sing "Kansas City" again. Then they invite Jessica in to do the scenes. Everything is going well. Trevor is excited about our scene work, I can tell. He looks at us, trying to come up with a note or a "fix" and then seemingly gives up with a happy smile saying, "Great. It's just great." I must mention, this is not like most auditions. Usually you can't tell what they are thinking. It's rare to be given such votes of confidence. By the time we got to singing the duet together I'm flying high. Nothing can go wrong. The notes he gives me I apply immediately. Jessica is right with me. It's a dream audition.

Afterward, Jessica and I take the elevator down together. It became clear that we both had felt the same energy in the room. In my mind, my chances on landing this role have shot up a great deal. After all, now I only have to dance for Stro.

FIFTEEN

MONDAY, MAY 7:

I wake up and remember what day it is. I rush to the living room and turn on New York 1 just in time to see *The Producers* receive fifteen Tony nominations. The run-down is as follows: Best Musical, Best Score and Best Book (Mel Brooks), Best Direction and

Best Choreography (Stro), Best Actor (two: Nathan and Matthew), Best Supporting Actor (three: Gary, Roger, and Brad Oscar), Best Supporting Actress (Cady), Best Orchestrations, Best Set Design, Best Costumes, and Best Lighting. We've beaten *Company*, which held the record at fourteen. I don't care about that. I'm just happy that Brad Oscar got a nomination. Last week, Michael Riedel did a full-page column in the *New York Post* on why Brad O. should be nominated for a Tony. I wonder if that helped focus voters on him? If so, great.

I have my first class today. I'm teaching tap at Broadway Dance Center. Thought I'd try to use all the "star power" I'm toting around these days. Actually, it goes back to my seeing Brother Fred. He reminds me of the importance of teaching and guiding young talent. Helping people reach their own goals. I may not be the best teacher in the world, but I'm not the worst either. I like to choreograph and challenge people. It's something I've been missing since I got to New York. So today we start.

FRIDAY, MAY 18:

It's an interesting time right now. We are all waiting for the Tony Awards, wondering what's going to happen. We're starting to feel a little of the backlash that Nathan and Matthew warned about. There are pieces about us every day in the newspapers, on television, in entertainment magazines. Folk in the biz are starting to get tired, I fear. Which could mean bad news for us on Tony night. The thing is, all of the hype that has been stirred up about us we seem to be living up to. It's not something that we are aware of. But people after the show keep saying to me, "I didn't think it could be as good as everyone was saying, but it was." I want to *see* the show now. It bums us all out that we can't. Here we are part of the biggest show in this town in years and we can't see it. Strange. I worry — what happens if we don't win all the things everyone predicts for us? Does the hype stop? Do ticket sales diminish? So often, you see shows that are the flavor of the month and then die a slow death. I would hate for that to happen. We've all worked too hard for that.

The Celebrity Issue

A constant throughout the run here (and even a bit in Chicago) are the celebrities that show up. During *How to Succeed*, Bill Ryall used to keep a log of who came. So I have started a list in my Handspring Visor of all the celebrity attendees that we know of.

As a child, I spent hours upon hours listening to Monty Python records, learning the skits and the British accents. I would perform the skits for family functions. Learning how to be funny. Fast-forward some eighteen years. I am using things I learned back then in a show that Eric Idle is now watching. Eric Idle. Never did I think I would have the chance to make *him* laugh. It was like being able to thank him for what he "taught" me. I didn't get to meet him, but knowing he was there was enough.

Now that we've opened it's even worse. There are at least two celebrities a night. Sometimes they come backstage. When Tommy Tune came someone mentioned that he had just gotten back from performing on a world cruise. Suddenly it hit me. The Manhattan Rhythm Kings. Wow. *"And the universe smacks Jeffry in the head on that one!"*

The night Connie Stevens and Joely Fisher came, they sat in the front row, laughing and making eyes at Matthew during the curtain call. They even sent us a basket of goodies the next day, signed "from the two crazy blondes in the front row."

Matthew and I get excited when the Mets or Yankees come. I get more excited over Yankees. Matthew is a pretty die-hard Mets fan. Todd Zeile and Benny Agbayani showed up, as did Joe Torre and Scott Brosius.

Best of all was when Gene Wilder came during previews. I came downstairs and there he was, coming through the stage door. He looked like a giant. An incredibly benevolent giant. He was very quiet and congratulated a few of us standing there. He went to Matthew's dressing room. I could only imagine how nervous Matthew must have been. Later he told me that Gene said, "You're very funny. You look tired, make sure you rest."

Hugh Jackman is a friend of Warren's. I asked Warren if I could meet him. I loved him in *X-Men*. Warren got him to sign a little white card to me. I don't usually do the autograph thing, but this was an exception.

Al Goldstein came. Now there's a poorly thought-out sentence. Al, if you don't know, is the man behind *Midnight Blue*, an adult TV show that plays on public access channels. Ray Wills and I happened to see him on the street in front of the theater, while we were on break during an understudy rehearsal. Apparently he was having trouble getting tickets. Go figure. So he had a deal going on his show where, if you got him tickets to *The Producers*, he would have an adult film star perform certain "acts" on you on his television show. I think Ray saw an opportunity, but, alas, Al already had tickets for the show. You know you've crossed cultural boundaries when Al Goldstein is trading oral sex with a porn star to get tickets for your show.

Some of the other notables: Tom Hanks, Joan Cusack, Martin Short, Stephen Weber, Jason Alexander, Paul Newman and Joanne Woodward, Billy Crystal, Mike Nichols, Jerry Stiller, Carol Burnett, Teri Garr, Carole King, Henry Winkler, Julia Roberts and Benjamin Bratt, Gene Hackman, Uma Thurman, Arthur Miller, Helen Gurley Brown, Sandy Duncan, Terrence McNally, Star Jones, and Horton Foote.

TUESDAY, MAY 29:

Steve Zweigbaum calls me today. He tells me that Nathan is going to be out and he can't find Ray Wills. He might have to put Brad Oscar on as "Max" and me on as "Franz." Whoa. He says it probably won't go down that way but wants to warn me just in case. Damn. I say, "Bring it on." But, 'twas not to be. Steve got a hold of Ray, who appeared in his first performance as Max Bialystock.

It's been obvious that Nathan's not doing well. His voice has been getting steadily worse with all the sickness going around. I'm glad he is taking time off. Our only worry was Tony voters. Have they all been here? If things were going to be tight between *The Full Monty* and us, this kind of thing could push it the wrong way. I find out at the theater that the voters have been notified and that they're waiting to come when Nathan gets back. So that's a relief.

Ray does a great job. During "Betrayed" when he sits down for "Intermission," he looks to his side as if talking to another patron and says, "I like the other guy better." And then continues the song. It got a laugh, but I felt bad for Ray. He doesn't need to say that. He did a great job.

The only problem arose when Matthew had to call him "Fat, Fat, Fatty." Ray is not fat. At all. So Matthew tried all sorts of things, like "Fat, fat fathead" and "Gimme those fat books, you kinda, sorta, not really fat guy." Over the course of four performances every one was different. It was then decided that Ray would have a fat suit made for him. He wore it in the last show, but it didn't make him look much fatter. Not sure what you do in that situation.

TONY, TONY, TONY, TONYYYYYY

SATURDAY JUNE 2:

The Tony rehearsal went as smoothly as our rehearsals usually do. The exciting thing was seeing Brad Oscar's cardboard sign that pointed out where he would be sitting. They do this so the cameramen can rehearse their shots when nominees are being announced. At the rehearsal, they go through the show award by award. The "winners" come up and give "acceptance speeches." These stand-ins are supposed to give a general idea of how long the speech will be. But most of them aren't talking nearly as long as most Tony winners talk. The director keeps telling them to talk more. On the winner cards, it said in bold print, "FOR THIS REHEARSAL ONLY . . . The 2001 Tony Award goes to . . . blah, blah, blah." Every stand-in had to say it. For the rehearsal, *The Full Monty* won for Best Musical. I wonder if that's some sort of omen.

At the start of this week I went to Barnes and Noble and saw a huge Tony Awards display. There was a book that detailed the winners, nominees, and all kinds of information on the Tonys since they started back in the 1940s. I brought it in and thought we could have some fun with "Tony Trivia." So, all week I have been forming questions for everyone downstairs between scenes. It started out as just the guys, but by midweek everybody was playing. My favorite style of question was "Give Me the Missing Nominee." I give them three names from the same category and year; they have to give me the fourth nominee. For example: "In 1987, these musicals competed for Best Musical — *Les Misérables, Me and My Girl, Rags*, and ???" For theater folk, that's an easy one: *Starlight Express*. So I tried to give them tougher ones. Abe was especially hard to stump. After being surprised a number of times by various people, I decided to really give them a tough one. "In 1985, these musicals competed for Best Musical — *Big River, Grind, Leader of the Pack*. Name the fourth nominee." Matt Loehr's eyes grew wide as he tried to find the answer. "I think I know this one," he said. I looked at Matt, being the youngest male ensemble member, and said, "What were you, two years old in '85? I don't think it's what you think." Yesterday, we had a long *Mystery of Edwin Drood* conversation, but it was never the answer to a question. So today I was purposely trying to fake them out.

DENNIS (one of our dressers): "Is it *Drood*?"
ME: "Nope."
MATT: "I know this."
ME: "I don't think you do, Matt."
ABE: "That's the year they eliminated Best Actor in a musical, right?"
ME: "Yes."
MATT: "Is it *Quilters*?"
Complete silence.
ME: (softly) "Yes. *Quilters*."
ROBERT: "*Quilters*?"
TRACY: "What the hell is *Quilters*?"
ME: "How did you know that?"
MATT: "I don't know. I just remembered it for some reason. I think that was the first year I watched the Tony Awards."

And from that moment on, everyone regarded Matt Loehr as the Tony Trivia Master.

SUNDAY, JUNE 3:

Well, today's the day. We have an early call at the theater for hair and costumes, then off to Radio City to run through our number, then back to the theater to do our matinee (3:00). After the show, I'm just going to stay at the theater until the Tonys. Our call is 9:00 and the Tonys actually start at 8:00. So rather than go home, I'll watch the TV in the swing dressing room until I have to get ready.

It's weird. We've been nominated for fifteen awards, yet I'm not sure how many of them the Broadway community wants us to win. Or will allow us to win. Sometimes in these "races," the voters will assume that everyone *else* is voting for one show (in this case *The Producers*) and will end up voting for something else. That's when the upsets occur. I think we'll have one or two like that. I can't see us winning all of them. The Broadway community doesn't like a sweep. They will try to spread it around as much as they can.

After the show, I grab some food and go back to the theater. It's only 6:30. I still have an hour and a half before the PBS part of the Tonys starts. I love doing the Tonys because you get to start watching it on TV, then you're on TV, then you go back to watching it again. It's freaky. This year I don't think we'll be able to watch anything afterward, though. We're next to last. Best Musical is given out after we perform.

At 8:00 a bunch of us gather upstairs. Matt Loehr, Brad Musgrove, and I begin the evening, and it grows from there. Christina and Adrienne come in to start their Old Lady makeup. The PBS portion begins. We laugh hysterically at Matthew and Nathan's hosting material. Matthew told me he was more worried about the opening stuff for the national broadcast than the PBS material.

First award is Orchestrations. Obviously we're rooting for Doug Besterman, but according to my doubts about how many awards the theater community would *allow* us to win, it's not a slam dunk. But win he did. And we all cheer. So happy for him.

The award for Choreography is next. This one we figure Stro has hands down. But you can never tell. She wins, and again we cheer. Now the awards for Book and Score, separately. First, Mel and Tom win for Book. We cheer. Mel starts his speech with "This is the hardest thing I've ever had to do . . . be humble." Everyone in the dressing room gasped. As his speech goes on, we get more and more worried about what else he's going to say. He finishes and the room is silent. Thankfully, there was a break in the award-giving action. We all look at each other.

CHRISTINA: We're winning *everything*, guys.
ME: I don't know about y'all, but I don't want to go out there after all this. They're going to hate us.
BRAD : I don't want to win any more Tonys!

We all laugh, but we feel the vibes. We hear the audience as *The Producers* is announced over and over. From our perspective, it seems that they are "turning." I'm afraid that by the time we get out there, rotten vegetables will be flying.

BRAD: How about that speech?
ME: You know, at first it made me nervous, but Mel doesn't have to apologize for this. He's celebrating it. And we all know how crazy he can be.
ABE: It's why the show is so funny. It doesn't apologize and he doesn't apologize.

We know that he's not trying to be pompous; he's trying to be funny and celebrate his accomplishment. He said what he was feeling, and he was feeling great. Congratulations, Mel.

Back at the awards, Robin Wagner heads up to accept his

award for Best Scenic Design. He looks so nervous we wonder if he's going to drop his award. His speech is heartfelt.

ABE: I think we got 'em back.

By the end of the PBS hour, we had taken every musical award. I caught the opening number (Melissa and the gang from *42nd Street*) of the national broadcast with Matthew and Nathan's opening dialogue. Matthew went off about how he was power hungry — a god, "even the moon fears me" — because the show was such a hit. Nathan brought him back to earth by reminding him about some of Matthew's movies that didn't do so well. We were all howling. Nathan and Matthew are the last people in the world to get "drunk with power."

Now we were getting ready for the show. Most of us are downstairs in Old Lady gear, getting our wigs on. Some doing makeup and stretching. TVs are on everywhere. A bunch of folks are in Matthew's dressing room watching, others in Wardrobe. I had to get my wig on. As Heather helps me, we hear people down the hall scream. We run into Matthew's dressing room and see that Cady has won for Best Supporting Actress. Minutes later, Gary wins for Best Supporting Actor. He starts his speech with "Heil Mel!"

A NOTE ABOUT GARY: From the time you meet him, you know you're going to like him. He greets you with a broad smile. He is as much in command of his talent as Nathan is. When he is performing, he is living. But Gary impressed me most by his incredible pursuit of his character. He would come in every day filled with ideas and takes on Roger DeBris. Never settling for the easy way out. He was constantly working at it. In a show like this one, where everyone (and I do mean everyone) is trying to get as many laughs as he can, Gary is a generous actor. He never gets in the way of someone else trying to create his or her own moment or laugh. He was so patient through the FDR thing. I know actors who would've signed off on that back in Chicago. When Gary won the Tony, there was justice in the world for once. Hard work had paid off. It's a story that emboldens you.

We assemble together upstairs and board the bus. A few fans are outside the theater cheering us on. We drive to the theater trying to watch the telecast on Ira's little remote around his neck. (Note to self: must get one of those.) We sit outside Radio City for what seems like hours. My blood sugar starts to drop like

Gary in his glory with the hotsy totsy Nazis. *L. to r., Bryn Dowling, myself, Gary Beach, Eric Gunhus, and Matt Loehr.*

crazy. I become desperate for something to eat. The bus driver happens to have a jar of applesauce, which he gives to me. So here I am, outside Radio City dressed as an Old Lady, spooning applesauce into my mouth. There's a New York memory.

Finally, we're let inside and stand ready backstage. I introduce myself to Dick Cavett. I compliment him on his work in *Rocky Horror*. Madeleine starts flirting with him in her "Hold Me–Touch Me" character. I calmly walk away.

As Nathan wins the Best Actor award he pulls Matthew out to accept with him. Classy.

We do our number without any veggie-throwing incidents. They *seem* happy to see us. After talking to some people in the audience that night, I got, from them, a feeling of complacency. Most people predicted that we were going to walk away with the awards but hoped there would be an upset or two.

After the number, we wait backstage. There's a side room with catered food and stuff. I feast. The applesauce had been used up long ago for adrenaline and I'm starving again. A few minutes later, we're back from commercial and Best Musical is about to be announced. I look over at Matt Loehr and say, "Tonight's Best Musical award goes to . . . *Quilters!*" We line up offstage. Waiting there, wondering what in God's name we will feel if we don't win. Glenn Close says, "They've broken the record, *The Producers!*" but we can't hear it from where we are. People behind me say, "Go! We won!" Ray, first in line, is still reluctant to go out, because he hadn't heard it himself either. But Kathy and I push him out, and we walk onstage as Mel and our producers are making their way up.

Mel takes the stand. Introduces — or tries to — all of the producers. Says a couple of funny things and we go to commercial. We all gather around Mel. I have the chance to shake hands with him. He says to me, "We did it, Jeffry Denman. We did it."

Nathan and Matthew come back onstage to say goodnight, and the director of the TV evening tells us to come downstage and join Mel, Nathan, and Matthew. During the final moments of the commercial break Nathan tells Mel he has to be quiet while they say goodnight. Just before we go back to "live," Mel drops his Tony, making a huge thud. The audience gasps, then starts laughing. Nathan grabs it away from him and we go back to live coverage. Nathan tells the viewers that Mel is "*still talking!*" and then does one of his "migraine headache" faints. The audience laughs again and we wave as the playoff music starts. When we get back onto the bus, I call my parents. They're throwing a Tony party, a first for them, and had wanted me to call as soon as I could. We get back to the theater and change. I call Melissa and congratulate her, and tell her I'll pick her up at her party. Because *42nd Street* took the only two awards we weren't up for (Best Actress and Best Revival) we realized that between the two of us, we represented every musical Tony Award. Pretty cool.

As I run through Times Square on my way to Laura Belle (where the *42nd Street* party is), I see the news ticker above ABC. It says we've *tied* the record for the most Tony Awards. I snap a picture, even though it's wrong.

I pick up Melissa at Laura Belle, and we head to the Bryant Park Grill. As we walk in, photographers start snapping our picture. Very Hollywood. We eat and shmooze and generally feel great about the evening. We head up onto the roof patio, where we find none other than Michael Riedel. He congratulates the both of us and we talk for a bit. Amazing how my impression of him has changed over the months. In cases like this, I like being wrong.

After a couple of hours, Melissa and I leave the party and stroll through Bryant Park. It's been an incredible day, week, month, half-year, year. That's the thing about this business. The highs are intense and they usually come without any warning.

They go quickly, too. But something tells me this one is going to be longer than usual.

Twelve awards. History has been made. It hasn't sunk in. Last night, I kept saying it aloud to come to some understanding of what the show had accomplished. I couldn't. Not with Mel Brooks standing next to me, saying it with me on the stage of Radio City, not with Susan Stroman saying it with me at the party afterward. Understanding never came. I was numb; trying to feel it or giving the impression of what I thought it should feel like. I was enjoying it, but the reality never compares to the imagination when you're outside of it. In the cab on the way home with Melissa, I said, "It feels like I'm still back in Buffalo at Upstage NY doing a summer show and everybody really, really liked it." Perhaps after all this hoopla is over, I will see it. I hope so. It is marvelous to think that you were part of history. And now I have been, twice. I thank God.

Oklahoma! *Dance Callback*

TUESDAY, JUNE 5:

It's been over a month since I last went in. I have been taking roping lessons, practicing my tours, my left pirouettes, my split leaps, everything I "hear" that Will does in Stro's version of the show. I go in with three other guys. Stro gives me a smile from behind the table. Warren is teaching the combination. He teaches us, very quickly, a fairly long and tricky combination, then has us do it one at a time. I can't say that I'm ready to do it by myself when Stro calls me up first. Remember how much I love going on first? Perfect. I do my best. I try to think of everything Trevor had told me about Will. How he's cocky, a showoff, and how he loves the attention he's getting from everyone. When you put me up against great dancers and judge me on technique, especially ballet, I will *never* win. But give me a story that you want me to tell and you won't notice that my technique's not perfect. I've never been a technician. I've always relied on my spirit and my acting to get me through. Well, I could tell right from the get-go that it wasn't working for them. I did it twice through as best as I could but knew that it wasn't what they wanted. But then again, I felt the same way after the Leo audition, so maybe I'm wrong.

Stro asks me about my roping skills. I show her some of my tricks, but even the rope seemed to be against me today. I managed to lasso Lisa Shriver, which they liked. But I walked out of there not feeling at all confident. The exact opposite of how I had felt after my audition for Trevor.

Sure enough, the call came through Ann. They're not considering me for Will anymore. I'm so frustrated. And I can't tell if it's with Stro for not giving me a second chance or with myself for not . . . I don't know, being better. Thank God I have a show to go to tonight.

The theater is electric today. There's that low hum of excitement again. Orchestra people congratulate crew members, dressers congratulate the hair department, it's wonderful. No conceit. No bragging. No taunting. Just pride and confidence.

Stro shows up before the curtain and congratulates us on the Tonys. I try to avoid her, but she comes over to me, gives me a hug, and says, "I was very proud of you today." All the reasons why I didn't do well start popping up in my head and threaten to become vocal. Quickly, I say thank you and shut my mouth.

We are saddened at the closing notices of *A Class Act*, *Bells Are Ringing*, and *Jane Eyre*. Everyone knows at least one person in each of the shows. It may sound Pollyanna-ish, but I hate it when any show closes. It bothers me. I think of being in *Dream* when

Tony, Tony, Tonyyyyyy. *Matthew Broderick (Leo Bloom), Nathan Lane (Max Bialystock), and Gary Beach (Roger DeBris) with (clockwise from bottom r.) Kathy Fitzgerald, Roger Bart (Carmen Ghia), Ray Wills, Peter Marinos, and myself.*

we got our closing notice after only four months. That was hard. People say, "It didn't find its audience." In some ways that's true. The first six months of a show on Broadway is primarily for those in the tri-state area. Your "other" real audience may be in Dubuque. You have to run awhile to "find" them.

During the performance, the audience stops the show with their applause after we sing "Tony, Tony, Tony, Tonyyyyyy" during "Keep It Gay." We were all taken aback. We didn't think they would make that connection quite so palpably.

FEELING A LITTLE "BOOKISH"

MONDAY, JUNE 25:

Back in Chicago, over dinner, Melissa and I had talked about the possibility of turning these journal entries into a book. It seemed like a good idea but I have no experience with anything of the sort. Fast-forward to today. Moments after I decide to go forward with it, an opportunity to meet with a publisher presents itself. Ann and Gene invite me over for dinner. We get to talking and I mention the material and tell them I'm trying to take the next step in having it published. Gene, it turns out, has cowritten three books on ragtime and jazz music. Gene thinks the idea is great and said that he would contact his editor.

TUESDAY, JULY 3:

Rick Dolan, the concertmaster (who plays the violin solos while I'm the Blind Violinist), had an accident today and is going to be out for at least a month. He was painting or something, on a ladder, and the ladder fell, injuring his hip and his bow hand. Rick and I connected early on, when I wanted to get his style for the violinist. His interpretation of the solos is great. We follow each other so well that people think I'm playing the violin up there. I hate to see something like this put him out. He loves the show and he loves playing. It's a delicate thing, the violin solos. One wrong move and the audience knows I'm faking it. Then I feel like a dork. Ashley (Rick's cover) did well tonight, but we weren't totally together. Which is to be expected.

I had an acupuncture session with a friend of Brad Oscar's. He saw the show a couple of weeks ago. He loved the show and the characters I play. At one point (no pun intended) he asked me, "So how long have you been playing the violin?"

THURSDAY, JULY 5:

I had my first of (I hope) many meetings with two editors at Routledge. They seemed intrigued. I gave them some excerpts. This is getting exciting.

Brother Fred

This evening I get together with Jim Deiotte ("Sing or blow me!"), Brother Fred, and some kids I went to high school with. Not kids anymore. Everyone has done well. The dinner is fun and relaxed and meaningful. When we get our drinks, I tell everyone the story of how I got *The Producers*. I reveal to Jim that it was all because I had used his famous line. He cracks up. He keeps saying, "I said that? I can't believe I said that! And you didn't tell me? How did I not get fired?" I thank him for teaching me how to get a Broadway show. In word, and in deed.

Fred is not doing well. A couple of years ago he was diagnosed with a rare heart condition. It leaves him more and more exhausted and so the time that we can spend together becomes less and less. Coming to the dinner tonight is a lot for him. It becomes clear that he has to get going. He goes to the men's room before we leave the restaurant, and, when he comes back, I can tell that he's been crying. I have never seen Fred cry. He looks at all of us, so proud. This table of young men represents what he has wanted to achieve with his life: to build strong, determined, and kind people who would pursue their dreams and become solid members of society, giving back as they had received. Here we were, a testament to Fred. I have a theory that Fred has spent his life giving his heart to all those around him. He doesn't have any left for himself.

FRIDAY, JULY 20:

Steve Zweigbaum stops me on the stairs today and tells me that Matthew is going on vacation in September and that Jamie and I will be splitting the week. I get Friday, Saturday, and Sunday. September 7, 8, and 9. I can't believe it. Wait, yes I can. I've worked my butt off. I call my parents right away. I tell them I don't care what they have to do, they're coming in. I call Ann to start figuring out who I need to get there. I wish I could go on once before that, so if I get really important business there, I'm ready. But then again, I know me. I'm going to be ready for whatever I have to do, be it one performance or four. I can't wait. Bring it on.

At dinner, I tell Jim Deiotte the good news. He says, "Get Fred there. Let him see you. Get your parents there, then Fred." I agree.

THE DOCUMENTARY SCREENING

TUESDAY, JULY 24:

I arrive from Buffalo this morning (I acted as godfather to my brother Bob's second child, Sarah. Very cool. I gave her a card with a picture of Marlon Brando as Don Corleone.), and I head to Sony on the East Side to watch a private screening of the documentary on the making of the recording of *The Producers*. I think my head just exploded. Mel is there. He announces that he and Tom Meehan are doing a coffee-table book on *The Producers*. My heart sinks. Then they show the program. It's good. Really gives an impression of what the day was like. Nathan's "interview with Mr. Brando" got cut down but was in there. The storm trooper tap recording section is nice. I got some nice time in there. My favorite part is at the end, where Nathan is saying goodbye to Mel on a staircase. Nathan looks at the camera and says, "Oh, this is the end of the documentary? This is where I say goodbye and then fall down the stairs." And then he does. Always on.

Later that day I talk to Gene Jones about the coffee-table book. He assures me, "Your book is totally different from what they're doing. Yours is a personal view of the events that happened. Don't worry. Just keep doing what you're doing. Both can exist together."

Last night I went on as the Lead Tenor in "Springtime for Hitler." The cool part was, I did my own track, then switched over to Eric's for "Springtime," then back to my own. Got to bow as Eric. It was cool. I wasn't all that worried about it beforehand. The thing that amazed me is how much my voice opened up when I started it. The only glitch was when I had to back up and present Gary. Eric has this riding crop thingy, and he casually puts it in his belt as he backs up. Well, I wasn't quite so casual about it. I couldn't find the top rim of my belt. Then my window of opportunity had passed, and I was in the freeze with the crop still in my hand. The next section of choreo requires that I have both hands available. So I tried nonchalantly to inch the crop

In my Lead Tenor costume.

back into my belt. It took what seemed like twenty minutes. The rest of the cast watched my struggle and laughed. *Finally* I got it in the belt. I can hear Warren's pen scribbling away on a white index card, "Jeffry — Riding crop a bit wonky." After "Springtime" Heather gave me the nicest compliment ever. I told her it was because of the hair. We had spent some time figuring out how I would look best as a Hitler youth. I was worried that my hair is not as blond as Eric's. She assured me that under the lights it looked lighter than usual. Ray Wills was especially supportive and complimentary after the number. There's nothing like the feeling of surprising people with your talents. Especially people who think they know what you do. Warren and I passed on the stairs after the show. I was excited. He asked, "How did you feel?" I cruised by him (gotta catch the A train) and said with a big smile, "Great. I don't remember any of it." He returned, "Don't worry, I've got it all written down," and he waved his white cards in the air. Robert, a few steps behind me, let out a big laugh. When I got to my space there was a single white index card at my place. It said: "Well done." That was all I needed. I met Melissa on the train and told her about the whole thing on the way home.

SATURDAY, AUGUST 4:

The documentary airs tomorrow. As I'm climbing the stairs after the first show, Jennifer and Madeleine are in front of me talking about an article on the film in the *Daily News*. It said, "The documentary works mainly because everyone is so joyful and because it was filmed before they knew what a phenomenon they were going to be." It would be fun to go back to those days just for a second to remind ourselves of the doubts that we had, just to keep us honest. Although I don't think anyone in our cast is buying into everything that the show has become. We know that Broadway is still Broadway. We know that eventually there will be "the job I did after *The Producers*" and we know that this business of show will continue to frustrate and excite us. At least I hope so. That's why I'm here.

A Typical Preshow Conversation

Things said backstage are often as funny as what's happening on-stage. A perfect example was tonight. Every night before the show the cast (minus Matthew, Gary Beach, and Roger Bart) stands onstage waiting to begin. Tonight, Matt Loehr, Brad Oscar, Madeleine Doherty, Nathan, and myself were standing together waiting for Ira's "Rock 'n' roll, gang," which tells us to get into places behind the Shubert set to start the show. This is when the funny stuff is said.

NATHAN: (to Matt Loehr) Are you wearing makeup?

MATT: Yeah, I put a little MAC cover-up on.

Nathan gives look of disbelief.

BRAD OSCAR: (to Nathan) What's wrong with that?

NATHAN: (to Brad) Do *you* wear makeup too?

BRAD: Yes, I put a little liner on.

NATHAN: (in amazement) Why?

BRAD: I have to bring out my features.

JEFFRY: (with loads of sarcasm) Yeah, 'cause you don't have a character face or anything.

NATHAN: Did you wear makeup when you went on for me?

BRAD (à la Norma Desmond): Yes! I wore lashes and lots of shadow . . .

NATHAN: White lipstick . . .

BRAD: It was fabulous.

NATHAN: You know, Matthew called me up at home when I was out, held the phone up while you were singing "King of Broadway," and said, "Here's what you're missing."

We erupt into laughter. The lights dim.

IRA: "Rock 'n' roll gang, rock 'n' roll."

TUESDAY, AUGUST 14:

Last week we received an invitation to attend a party at Sardi's for Tom Meehan today. He's getting hung up! This will be my first Sardi's hanging party. What an honor. Tom definitely deserves it. I wonder if they will be putting Mel up? Maybe he's already there somewhere. It'll be nice to see everyone. We haven't had a social gathering in a while.

FRIDAY, AUGUST 17:

Been thinking about the "Matthew week," as I am calling it. Suppose I should call it "Bloom week," since of course I'm not really going to be Matthew. I'm trying to get some casting people there, as well as family and friends. Brad, Roger, Cady, and Gary have been great about helping me with extra house seats. My parents are coming for the last show. Ann will be there Friday and Saturday night with casting folk. My brothers and their wives will be there Saturday night, along with others I've invited. Talk about coming full circle, I've invited Michael Riedel from the *Post*. He was excited about my going on, said he'd love to come, and said we should have dinner afterward. "We western New Yorkers gotta stick together." Holly, my masseuse, is going to come in between shows on Saturday to give me a between-show massage. Be jealous, be *very* jealous. I am planning a party on Sunday night for my family and friends.

Now for the real stuff. How worried am I? Medium. But that's good for me. Again, as always, it keeps me honest. I know my stuff. I've just never had to do a part this size on Broadway before. Munk was a big role, but this is different. My biggest concern is Nathan. This is his show. Especially that week. He has a rhythm and he doesn't like change. He's Nathan. He's allowed. Excluding the folks I've invited, no one in the audience is going to be there to see me. That will be a prominent issue. I've heard people "vocally comment" when they announce that Matthew's not in (both here and at *How to Succeed*). I've watched audiences not laugh because it's not Matthew doing the bit. This is going to be tough, no doubt. I figure if I just do what I know, keep it fast and funny, don't get in Nathan's way, and try to enjoy myself, I should be okay.

I have been watching Matthew this past week like an eagle. The most important thing to me is keeping the rhythm of the show going. I said to Melissa today, "It's like making dinner. When I first go out there Friday, I'm not going to be attempting any gourmet meals. I'm going to reheat what I've kept frozen from understudy rehearsals. We'll see how that goes. Maybe on Saturday or Sunday, I'll try and add some spices."

SATURDAY, AUGUST 18:

I came home tonight to a message from Mel in regards to a letter I had dropped off at his apartment. William Germano, my editor, said that we had to make sure that it was okay with Mel that we do my book. So I decided I would write him a letter. He called today in response to it, saying that he was happy that I was taking on this endeavor, I was not incurring any wrath from him, and that he'd love to read any parts that pertained to him so he could check it all out. I was bouncing off the walls. He said the loveliest things at the end. I am going to keep that message for a *long* time.

Dancing Topless on David Letterman's Desk

WEDNESDAY, AUGUST 22:

After the first show I'm up in my dressing room. I get a page over the monitor. "Jeffry Denman, you have a phone call in the stage manager's office." I figure it's Mel calling to tell me what he thought about the manuscript excerpts I had sent him. That's the only person I could imagine calling me at the theater. It turns out to be Bill Coyle, from PR. He tells me that the *Letterman* show needs a body/dance double for Dave, and my name had been given. I immediately call the show. A woman named Jill Leiderman tells me that Jonathan Dokuchitz (a fellow cast member from *Dream*) has recommended me, and she would love it if I could come over and do a post-tape shoot. She promises to have me back by the second show. I say sure. I run over to Daniela's (a restaurant that Melissa and I frequent), where Melissa is entertaining one of her dance teachers, who had just seen *42nd Street*. I tell her the news and then run over to the Ed Sullivan Theatre.

After waiting around a bit, Jill comes and gets me, along with two very buff, tan, good-looking model types. I get nervous. I know my type. That ain't it. Often you find yourself in an audition situation where a friend has recommended you for a job without knowing exactly what they are looking for. You show up and you're the only Jim Carrey in a room full of Mark Wahlbergs. That's when the business sucks. I was hoping this wasn't one of those times.

We go downstairs underneath the stage to audition for Jill. Above us, they are taping tonight's show. The premise of the bit is that a fan has sent in a letter saying, "Dear Dave, can I be the first man to dance topless on your desk?" And then Dave says, "I'm sorry, but someone has beat you to it." Then they roll tape and you see a man dancing topless on Dave's desk (head cut off) with a ticker on the bottom of the screen that says, "Tom Brokaw," then a second clip with a heavier man with the ticker saying, "Al Gore." The third topless celebrity they hadn't settled on yet. Jill wants me to be Tom Brokaw *and* Dave and asks if I can do a little stripper dance for her. She wants to see what the other two guys can do too. One of the models has a problem dancing with no music. I suggest we wait for a commercial break, when Paul Shaeffer plays a long stretch of music. Jill turns to me and says, "Brilliant." I don't think the idea is all that brilliant, I just think that she's too frazzled from making decisions all day and is glad someone else is.

So we get to a commercial break, and the music starts. One of the models and I start grinding and swaying. The other model (the one who didn't want to dance without music), looks confused, but starts moving around.

> JILL: (to the troubled model) Can you dance like you're stripping for someone?
> TROUBLED MODEL: Where are they?
> JILL: In front of you.
> T.M.: What do you mean?
> JILL: Well, like there's someone in a chair in front of you.
> T.M.: Well, can you get a chair and have someone sit in it?

I look over at the other model, who is doing a very nice job, and give him a look like, "Is this guy for real?" Dude, just pretend. We're in the basement of the Ed Sullivan Theatre taking our shirts off and squirming around for a talent coordinator while production assistants and stagehands run by. Sometimes you just have to make do.

> JILL: (completely speechless)
> T.M.: Oh, you want me to pretend.

Riiiiiiight. Now the commercial break is over and the band stops playing. Perfect.

I go upstairs to call Steve Zweigbaum to see how much time I could get. Jill had said that, depending on who I played (she had me slated to dance as Tom Brokaw and Dave, pending the writers' approval), they might run close to 7:30. No answer at the theater. When I come back she's made her decisions. The guy who'd had such a problem pretending is kept for Dave and I'm still Tom. I feel bad for the other guy. We're whisked up to the costume room and start putting on appropriate clothing. Within minutes I'm whisked back down to the stage and am being introduced to the director. He asks me to take off my shirt, get up on the desk, and try out some stuff. After a short rehearsal on the desk Dave walks in. He looks at me and says, "Hello, there. Thanks for doing this." I laugh and say, "Don't thank me yet." He smiles and sits down. I couldn't help but think that one day, if David Letterman ever interviews me, they'll still have this footage. That could be a problem.

We shoot the clip, I thank Dave, Jill, and the rest, and I'm whisked up to the costume room again. When I get back to the St. James I'm in a daze. It had all happened so quickly. You just don't wake up in the morning and think, "Gee, I wonder if I'll be on *Letterman* tonight." Before I left Jill asked me to drop off a picture and resumé. I'll do that tomorrow. I told her I'm a good tap dancer. She's been looking for a tap-dancing Dave. I hope she calls.

Misadventures and Helicopters

SATURDAY, AUGUST 25:

I have been keeping Matthew and Nathan's antics out of the journal for a while now. Mainly because (1) they happen quite often, and (2) the feeling is hard to reproduce in writing. But I am now going to attempt because tonight was a classic.

We started with a so-so crowd. They were a bit tough, especially the woman in the front row who scowled at us the whole night. Like she was saying, "I heard you were funny. So come on, be funny!" We got to the part of the show where Nathan tells Matthew the "two cardinal rules of being a Broadway producer. . . ." For some reason, this has become a place where Nathan consistently has trouble staying with "the show." Try as he might, he looks at Matthew standing there with that silly grin on his face, and he busts. Usually it takes him two or three attempts to get through the "two cardinal rules" line. Eventually he'll get it and move on. Tonight it was quite different.

He got to the line and started laughing, putting his head on Matthew's shoulder. The audience didn't get what was happening. Which was par for the course that evening. After Nathan repeated his line, they figured out what was going on. Now the ad-libs start between he and Matthew. These are sometimes funnier than what is written (which is why Stro "discourages" them from going there.) The audience gets such a kick out of the fact that they have dropped character. It's that "behind the scenes" feeling. They love it.

Anyway, after a few failed attempts at getting through the "cardinal rules" line without laughing, Nathan walked over to the couch and laid down, saying, "I'm just gonna have a nap." The audience laughed. Then he said, "Where did they take Mariah Carey? That's what I want to know." The audience roared. (Mariah's breakdown and rehab is very big in the news today.) Backstage we were all watching. So far, this was normal. He got back up. Finished the line with Matthew, amid laughing and tears. Then he walked to the back of the "office," opened the bay window/doors, and jumped out the window. (What he really did was jump into the air and fall on the floor. The couch masked the fact that he was lying on the floor. It looked as though he had gone out the window.) Then, unseen by the audience, he crawled back in behind the couch, climbed to his feet, and said, "It's okay.

It was only one floor down." The crew, cast, stage managers, and, of course, the audience were split wide open. This was the craziest thing he had done. In a way, it seems he has to do this kind of stuff for himself. His mind is constantly going, and he has to shake things up just to stay sane. There are people who have a problem with what he does. I don't. It's live theater. We should be glad we have someone as good as Nathan doing the ad-libs.

TUESDAY, AUGUST 28:

I get a call from my friend, Luis Villabon. He's Paula Abdul's assistant on *Reefer Madness*, which opens Off Broadway this fall. Apparently she needs some bodies to work with in a studio, so Luis asks me if I'm interested. I tell him yes and volunteer Melissa as well. We meet at New Dance Group and proceed to work with them for about four hours on various parts of the show. I was about sixteen when I *really* started dancing. Paula Abdul was the hottest thing at that time, and I watched her videos and tried to mimic the moves therein. When I went to college, her style was still the rage, so that's what we learned in jazz class. A part of me is in sync with her style, although I never really became fluent that way. It's a lot of work and very hard on your body. Today, I'd rather tap and do the elegant stuff. That's more me.

Anyway, we begin work on some pretty easy musical staging. She lets us play around a bit, then she forms it into something. Halfway through the day I find myself doing a combination *with* her. It's all pretty easy, but dancing next to her and doing hip rolls with the queen of gyration is a real trip. In times like this, I thank God that I'm doing what I'm doing. And that the path I'm on continues to offer such gifts to me. I will never take these things for granted.

At the end of the day I ask Luis if Paula would be interested in coming to see me as Leo. She's not sure about her rehearsal schedule, but she's excited about it and she says, yes for now. I tell her I'll need a definite by the 1st. It'd be great if she could come.

At the show tonight things get interesting even before the curtain goes up. At half hour, Matthew isn't there. He usually arrives right on time. On occasion, I've come through the stage door at half hour with him right behind me. But for the most part he's dependable. Abe comes into our dressing room and says to Warren, "So, is Matthew in yet?" No one knew what he was talking about. Apparently, Matthew had spent the day out in the Hamptons. On his trek back into the city, he found that the Long Island Expressway had become basically a parking lot. Time was ticking away. So he did what? He hired a helicopter. A helicopter. And he ends up making it in time for curtain. I can't even imagine how you go about doing that. Can most people? Do you run to the nearest airport and say, "Hi, I'm Matthew Broderick. I need a helicopter." I don't know. I'm dying to ask him.

In the accountants' scene tonight when Matthew looks over at me after his briefcase comedy, I make the soft sound effect of a helicopter: "chukka, chukka, chukka, chukka." At first he doesn't know what I'm doing, then he realizes what it is and laughs.

Ann has successfully gotten some industry people to commit to attending my Leo Bloom performances. I'm glad. Who knows if it will do any good? I'm hoping it will at least increase awareness. These things are always tricky.

WEDNESDAY, AUGUST 29:

Harry Groener was in the audience tonight with his wife Dawn! I didn't see them until the curtain call. I caught his eye during "Goodbye!" Dawn waved and Harry just smiled a big grin. After the show I raced down to find him. I didn't know if he would be coming backstage. I found him at the stage door with Gary Beach. He gave me a big hug and said the nicest things about the show. Dawn finished talking to Gary and came over and did the same. There's something about Harry that Heather, my hair person, said to me. When he gives you a hug, he really hugs you. So many times, you give someone a hug and you can feel that they're not in it or thinking about something else. Harry doesn't do that. He hugs you full on. He lets go only when he's *done* hugging you. I love that. Just seeing his smiling face and talking to him for a few minutes was such a great energy hit. He wished me the best with the show. Didn't once talk about what he was doing. I had to pry info out of him, even though I follow what he's doing. I am going to write a show for him and me someday.

Backstage Rituals

Theater folk are a superstitious lot. There are tons of theater taboos. One of the most famous is exemplified in our song: "It's Bad Luck to Say Good Luck on Op'ning Night." Most of these superstitions have grown old, and their "power" has faded a bit. But actors today, as in the old days, love the rituals we make during a show. You don't even mean to create them. They start innocently, something you do on a whim that brings a laugh or a smile. The next night you see that person again, and you repeat it, trying to repeat the laugh. By the third night, it has become a ritual that you will do until you leave the show. God forbid you forget one night. Or you're sick and you didn't tell your understudy to do it.

The backstage rituals and events keep the show from becoming monotonous. Even the most devoted cast member can have a day when the routine may get to him or her. Knowing that you and your dresser are going to do that little dance the next time you have a costume change can help you make it to that change. Mind you, these are not world-changing events. But they are part of the fabric of the theater and are as individual as the people who create them. Here are a few of my backstage rituals.

Gathering and Greeting the Gentlemen

Before every show, without fail, I stop by the crew area, a small room offstage left, and enter with "Gentlemen!" Barnie answers with "Sir!" Then I give them a nugget of knowledge or a quote or just a word of encouragement. All done with a British accent because I'm dressed in a tux. Don't ask me why, these things just evolve. My favorite day was when Tim and Richie were watching the horse races and the trumpet tattoo sounded that tells the jockeys the race is starting. Richie said it would be nice if that little tune had lyrics. The next day I came in with some salty lyrics, which I will not quote here. All of this began with "Gentlemen!" Behind this ritual of mine is my admiration for what our stagehands do every day. They work their butts off. The intermission changeover is the most intricate dance of bodies (human and Nazi puppet), props, and set pieces I have ever seen. For that, I wish them luck and thank them daily.

Sugar

Before we start the opening number, the ensemble is set behind the "Shubert" set piece. I am standing with Naomi and Angie. I give each of them a kiss on both cheeks before we go out, usually saying, "Gimme some sugar." You might think this is inconsequential, but there have been times when Naomi has given me a look of concern because our entrance is coming and I haven't doled out the kisses. In Chicago, Michaelangelo, the Renaissance wrestler, would watch as I gave kisses to the girls. One day he said, "Where's mine?" (Now I know what prison feels like.) At first I thought he was kidding. The next day I gave him kisses. Instant ritual.

Cue 47

This is a ritual I am not a part of but watch. During Max and Leo's first scene together, Leo says the magic words, "a producer could make more money with a flop than he could with a hit." There is a musical cue, called a sting, after he says that. On the sting Max sits up, letting the audience know that the idea has been hatched. Offstage left, the men are getting ready on the accountants' palette. The platform fits so tightly that one of the file cabinet doors opens right next to the stage manager's dais. Every night, Matt Loehr goes behind the palette and opens the door right on the musical sting, which, coincidentally, is cue 47 in the stage manager's logbook. It started out just as a small little "grand entrance." Now he has themes. Sometimes he enters with a prop, like a machine gun from "Springtime." Or the black cat that Max throws into the stage door in Act Two will come through the door like a Muppet on *Sesame Street*. Sometimes he even gets other actors to play along. He once held Peter Marinos hostage, threatening Casey (the stage manager) by saying, "I want my personal day, I want my personal day!" All of this to entertain the stage manager who is calling the show. It's something they look forward to.

Three

This started in Chicago. In "I Wanna Be a Producer," toward the end, the accountants reenter on the rolling palette and sing two "unhappy"s, a long string of "very"s, finally ending on "sad." When we began to tech the number, the platform and the musical phrase weren't lining up. So Glen and Patrick added "so unhappy" after the first two "unhappy"s. When you have been singing something for over six weeks one way and you have to make a tiny, little, subtle change, it can drive you (and your musical director) crazy. Every night, at least one of us would forget.

So Matt and I started to look at each other before the entrance and hold up three fingers to remind ourselves. It worked. It still does. Now it's more of a ritual than anything else. The scene doesn't go as well if one of us forgets. I'm sure of it.

Peter's Dream Ballet

During "When You Got It, Flaunt It" the ensemble are downstairs changing into Old Lady gear. Peter Marinos takes this opportunity to put on his own cabaret show for us. He uses the long hall as a runway and swishes and sways, mouthing the song's lyrics while deftly getting into his dress and wig.

Peter Marinos flaunting it.

"Haben Sie Gehoert" Backup Dancers

I don't remember when this started or who started it. It just evolved. Jennifer Smith might be the culprit. While Brad Oscar is singing the first bridge of "Haben Sie Gehoert Das Deutches Band" there is a group of about eight of us (including stage managers and crew) who replicate the choreography Brad is doing onstage. You are frowned upon if you miss it. There was a week when my back was injured and I was doing costume changes as slowly as I could. Jennifer Smith came up to me after I missed three days and said, "The group is concerned that you've been missing our sessions." I explained the reason. She said, "Well, that's fine, but please know that you are expected to be back there once you're healed. It doesn't set a good example if people start slacking off, you know." Remember, this is *backstage*.

Sweet Taters

This is pretty basic, but, if it *doesn't* happen, the show isn't worth $100 a ticket. More like $98.35. Before we go out for "Bavaria" (the beginning of "Springtime") Robert, Kathy, and I are offstage right. Robert and I hit our fists together, which we called "taters." We did this simply and calmly until Kathy started to get in the way. Trying to be funny, she would get her hands in the middle of our moment. This led to our shoving her out of the way, doing taters farther offstage when she wasn't looking. One time, before we had successfully achieved "tater-status," the music cue sounded. We went onstage in the dark and set up. We all got into our positions and froze. That's when I felt Robert's hand let go of mine, give me a small "tater," and then grab my hand again for the pose. The curtain went up and we started singing. Gotta do it. In Chicago, this evolved into "Sweet Potaters" after a fabulous meal at Redfish, a Cajun restaurant we frequented. Robert and I liked the sweet potatoes so much that we renamed our ritual after them. That's some good 'taters.

FDR Change Whip

This started with my dresser, Gay, in Chicago, then transferred to my new dresser, Kelly, in New York. During the "Heil-Lo" section of "Springtime" (where five members of the ensemble come downstage and sing tight harmonies as Gary dances around), there is a sound cue for a whip crack. At this point I am offstage right doing my quick-change into FDR. Whatever I am doing at the time, I stop and make a huge arm gesture as if cracking a whip. Sometimes, if it's the end of a two-show day and I'm tired, Kelly will help me out and do it with the yellow tie around my neck. It gets us through the last stretch of "Springtime." She likes when I dance it up a bit.

Sugar Fix

This is the most dangerous of our show rituals. Dangerous because of what happens when it *doesn't* take place. As Matthew and Cady are dancing off after "Leo Goes to Rio," I am set stage left getting ready to enter as the guard in the "Betrayed" scene. When we started in Chicago, I would stand at attention as Matthew passed. He would give me a salute or an "at ease" or whatever, just screwing around. Then I started doing things with props as they passed. Trying to make them laugh. Then one fateful day in New York, I brought them each a piece of chocolate. I put one piece in each hand and had them pick the hand they wanted. When I went home for Sarah's christening I missed a Sunday-afternoon show. When I came back on Tuesday, Ira told me that Cady and Matthew were upset that there was no candy on Sunday. When they came off, they said, "You need to tell the swings about this." Ira said, "We'll put it in the Show Bible." (The Show Bible is the definitive manual that stage management keeps that defines all technical cues, music cues, actors' lines and crosses, even choreography. Basically, whatever makes the show run.) You get used to that sugar fix every day at the same time. Just doing my part to keep dentists employed.

CHARACTER ASSASSINATIONS

That's hardly true. Every person involved in this show deserves to be recognized for what he or she brought to the table. Every person had a moment of inspiration at some point in the process that helped the show along. Helped it to be funnier. I wish I could write about all of them. But doing that, I think, would trivialize, a bit. However, working with the "Big Five" was something that I will treasure always and I feel, now that I've had some time with them, I can address that here.

Nathan Lane

How to get a blind violinist's attention. *Nathan Lane (Max Bialystock) and myself.*

I'll start with Poppa. That's what he calls himself at the theater. When Stro set the Blind Violinist bit with Nathan and me I couldn't have been happier. Mainly because it was the top of the show and it was one of the first bits. I was glad to have the honor. Being next to Nathan onstage for any length of time energizes you. I have never had any trouble getting inspired for the theater. But Nathan compels me to do my best. No, better than my best. Because that's what he does. He gives everything he has to the audience. He may get upset if they aren't responding but he will always try to win them over. People come to watch him in a show or a movie and they see only a part of Nathan's true talent. That just goes to show, I think, how talented he is. The aspect of Nathan that is fascinating to me is his mind. His quick brain can think of the wittiest thing to say at any moment. To be with him in a rehearsal room, when he is riffing off the other actors, especially Matthew, is thrilling and exhilarating. Or watching him onstage while something goes awry. He deftly comes up with the perfect comment to let the audience in. He has such determination and command. What could be more wonderful to watch eight times a week? Sure he breaks every once in a while, but even then he is trying to devise a way of getting the audience to get with him. And you don't fault Jerry Rice for dropping one pass when he scores four touchdowns in a game.

Matthew Broderick

Though I knew Matthew from *How to Succeed*, I can't say I got to know him well back then. I was a swing, which meant that the only times he saw me, someone was "out" or sick. Now I have "graduated" and am creating my own stuff. I like to think that we have connected a bit now. For all the fame, and the bullshit that seems to come with it, he keeps a level head. He's kind to his fellow cast members. He's kind to his fans, but he knows when to say no to them. He works hard and likes to enjoy his life. He loves to laugh. He has a remarkable ability to access film quotes at a moment's notice. Seldom have I seen him at a loss when the right quote from the right film will make everyone laugh. People watch him when he comes into a room. Friends and strangers alike. Staring at him, waiting for him to do something funny. He always complies. His physical comedy is astounding. I'm not sure people truly appreciate what he does as Leo, but as his understudy and as a dancer, I can tell you he is one of a kind.

Susan Stroman

Part of me feels that my entire performing life has been leading me toward working with Stro. I wonder if we'll work together again. She wants her actors to be triple threats. That is all I have ever tried to be. Nothing would please me more than to be a vehicle for her interpretations. But she tends not to ask about that at auditions. My career has always been something that took care of itself. I show up and do my best and try to let go of any control I mistakenly think I have. Things generally fall into place. They happen the way they're meant to. So Stro and I will meet again if were supposed to, I guess. Very Zen, huh? As far as this experience is concerned, I came into it almost fearing her. I am confident that she did finally "see" me. She appreciates what I bring to the show. I wish I knew her better. You can't help but want to be her friend. The tragic story of her husband, the director Mike Ockrent, often comes to mind when I think about her. There is sadness behind her laughter and her genius. I can't begin to imagine how she deals with that, but she does. And she creates happiness where she goes. She loves the theater and the theater loves her.

Tom Meehan

The unsung hero, Tom Meehan is quiet and soft-spoken. It seems that, with Tom, it's not about the fame, it's about the story. The work. He will tell you that he didn't do all that much, that he just helped Mel with a joke or two here and there. But Tom did much more than that. And Mel gives him credit for it. Mel told us the first day that Tom told him when the play had to sing. For a musical — for this musical especially — that's where the gold is. If your show isn't singing in the right places, by the right people, about the right things, it's not going to be a hit. All the right people came together at the right time in *The Producers*. Mel says he couldn't have done it without Tom. So Tom Meehan is as guilty as the rest of us.

Mel Brooks

"I can't believe you know Mel Brooks!" That has been the phrase of the year. For a while I couldn't believe it either, but now I do. From shaking my hand the first day of rehearsal, to screaming at me to make funnier noises as FDR, to dancing with his wife while I sang at Petterino's, to being with him onstage at the Tony Awards, my time with Mr. Brooks has been a wild ride. It wasn't always comfortable, but the best roller coasters aren't either. I once asked him privately, "What constitutes a funny noise?" He sternly replied, "I can't tell you how to be funny. Either you are or you aren't." It was hard to hear, but it's true. That's the essence of Mel: he tells the truth. (People don't always want to hear it.) And for that, I love Mel. He gives freely. When he is happy, there is no one more joyful. When he is not, his anger comes from not being able to articulate the things that are flying around in his head. People often say that about geniuses. I hope I've learned to be funny. But I know I've learned one thing: "If you don't have anything funny to say . . . shut up until you do."

THREE DAYS TO GO

TUESDAY, SEPTEMBER 4:

Tick tock tick tock. Melissa and I went to New Hampshire to visit her parents for Labor Day. We left Sunday after the show and came back this afternoon. It was a great way to get my mind off the coming week, but today as I get back into the city I realize that half the week is gone. I am still trying to get some casting/business people to the show. It's been harder than I thought. I have some coming on Friday and Saturday. I thought that the opportunity for tickets to the show would be enticing enough, but most of the casting folk have already seen it. And I imagine that Matthew *not* being in it isn't overly thrilling to them. Oh, well. I'm trying not to get upset about it. Whatever's going to happen will happen, and I've gotten a number of people to commit. (I'm not going to print their names here yet for fear of jinxing it.) Next Monday, September 10, I will do my final entry and all will be revealed then. That's the other clock that's ticking down. Monday marks the end of this journal. I'll have gone on as Bloom.

Jamie did well going on for Matthew tonight. He was nervous, but got his feet under himself quickly. Looks like he had some family and friends here. It's a great thing to see people in the audience crying and laughing during the curtain call. You could tell who was there for him. That's a great feeling.

Turns out that all of my aunts and uncles are coming to see me this weekend. Melissa's mom, Martie, is coming in too. Familywise, nobody left out. Sure, I'd love for all of my cousins to be there. But with the ticket situation, I was glad to get my aunts and uncles. Can't tell you how good that's going to be for the family get-togethers.

All tonight, I've been edgy. I have so much energy. I'm surprised that it hit me so soon. Guess I can feel it coming. I've been prepping for this so long that I can't believe it's actually here. My technique for dealing with it is simple: try to create the circumstances I will be faced with over and over so that I'm used to it. For example, I do the Leo scenes backstage while the show is going, so that I can match the pacing and energy that Nathan and the rest of the cast are used to. That way I know where the laughs, pauses, and everything else lie. I also plan for disaster. There is nothing worse than pausing for a laugh that never comes. I know I am not Matthew Broderick and never will be. When I walk out onstage I *don't* have ten movies that people can draw on while they watch me. Audiences laugh more when Matthew does crazy things because they feel they know him. They are rooting for him before they get to the theater. They are dying to see him. That is something no actor who is not well known can have. You can only go out and try to win them over. And you do that, I think, by keeping the energy up, by telling the story, and by doing what you know how to do.

As Leo, I'm lucky because Nathan does the heavy work. That is why I am focused on staying with him, making sure I keep throwing the energy back to him. God, I sound like Acting 101. But these basics keep me steady. Yes, I have to be funny. Yes, I have to be quirky and nerdy. But in the end, the show is a comedy and it has to move. Jokes have to be set up and knocked down like bowling pins. My job this weekend is to (1) not get in the way of that, and (2) be my charismatic, energetic self. Oh, and modest, too. Be the guy who loves performing. Enjoy my time out there. Because that's what has always made people watch me. I sound egotistical here, but let me go there for a second because this is a huge week for me. The only way I can do what I have to do this weekend is to prop myself up good. I know I am talented, but this weekend there will be four audiences full of people who are upset that Matthew is not in the show, which means that winning them over will be hard. And believe me, you can feel it onstage. The only way it won't affect your show is if you know deep down who you are and what you have to offer. My place on earth is not to be Matthew Broderick's understudy. This is a step along the way. I have been given an opportunity to shine, and I'm going to grab it by the handles. This is life right now. In the midst of performance there is no before or after. It's all in the moment. The classes, the auditions, the work. It all culminates this Friday, Saturday, and Sunday.

ONE DAY TO GO

THURSDAY, SEPTEMBER 6:

T-minus one and counting. I have a put-in rehearsal with the principals tomorrow. I have a photo shoot today, posing in the slide from "That Face." I am nervous as all get-out and can't sit still. Yesterday was a very intense day. Still more attempts to get casting folk to see me in the show. I was treated very rudely on the phone yesterday morning. It amazes me how some casting directors and their assistants treat actors — actors, who are *the only reason they have a job*. I know there are a lot of us, but that doesn't give them the right to treat us like shit. That said, there are casting directors who are great. Julie Hughes, who sadly has retired from casting, was always kind and polite to actors. Tara Rubin will take my calls more often than not. Same with Vinnie Liff and Geoffrey Johnson (who spells his first name wrong; see cover of this book for correct spelling). And I'm not saying that because they cast *The Producers*. They have *always* been very kind and respectful.

A couple of years ago, I was cast as Rueben in a tour of *Joseph* through Johnson-Liff. Two days later, I was offered a Broadway job (principal cover/swing in *Dream*). Even though I'd be turning down a principal role for a swing job I thought I should stay in town and do the Broadway gig. Vinnie totally understood. He was upset, but he understood and never held it against me in future auditions. Vinnie always calls me in and supports my attempts to move into the "principal world." Anyway, enough of that rant. I have people coming, and I should just be happy with that.

I had errands to run today. Just busy stuff, part of which involved my walking by the Winter Garden. It was appropriate since I had gotten an e-mail from Fred earlier today. He reminded me of all that had happened in the course of a year. One year ago I was getting ready to close *Cats*. My final entry in this journal will be on the one-year anniversary of that event. It's crazy how life works that way. As I walked by the Winter Garden, I visualized the amazing places life had taken me since I last exited those doors. I crossed the street and went inside. John the doorman, ever faithful, was still there. "Hey, there!" he said. I asked if I could take a look around and he said yes. It's amazing what they've done. They have spent the year gutting the theater and refurbishing the lobby and audience area. It's gorgeous. According to one of the workmen, they have tried to replicate the original colors of the theater. As I walked around, I tried to picture *Cats* and the garbage and the crowds and the confetti, but I couldn't. *Cats* was gone. And just as we had taken over the St. James and whisked out *Swing!* with our new energy, *Mamma Mia!* was poised to do the same at the Winter Garden. You could feel it. Part of me was glad. It was good that there was nothing left. Clean break. Funny that it took me a year to get it. But I couldn't help feeling a bit nostalgic for the old energy of *Cats*. I'm glad that the memory hasn't faded. (I can't believe I actually wrote that.)

At the show tonight I'm more nervous than ever, constantly saying to myself, "Tomorrow night I'll be somewhere else, tomorrow night I'll be in my dressing room, tomorrow night I'll be singing the solo. . . ." On and on and on. Everybody has been great this week, so generous with the good wishes. At the top of Act Two, Angie and I dance "That Face" together backstage. We usually do it the night before understudy rehearsals. This is different. By the end, adrenaline is coursing through me, saying, "What do you mean we have to wait till tomorrow night? Damn!" I even get a bit choked up, thinking about tomorrow.

During intermission I'm called to the stage manager's desk. Steve tells me that Nathan is extremely tired and doesn't want to come in for my put-in rehearsal tomorrow. (A put-in is exactly what it sounds like. You are "put in" to your role with all of the rest of the cast.) Steve asks if I'm going to be okay without it. I tell him it's fine, but I'm freaking inside. But then I figure, if Nathan trusts me enough to forgo rehearsal, that's a good sign. I'll be able to surprise him a bit with what I'm going to do. Might give him a jolt of energy, make him feel a little better. Steve and I will run lines at 3:30 tomorrow. I'll get together with the girls for "I Wanna Be a Producer," then I'll dance with Cady. The rest of the time I'll just continue freaking out.

Melissa and I meet on the subway platform and head home. Have our usual dinner, Shake 'n' Bake chicken with Rice-a-Roni. Comfort food. Now I'm writing, trying to tire myself out so I can sleep. I hate to say goodnight because that means tomorrow is pretty much here.

The Day

FRIDAY, SEPTEMBER 7:

Morning

It's déjà vu all over again. The day I had my callback for *The Producers*, I couldn't sleep. I haven't been able to sleep for three days. And the feeling in my stomach is the exact same. This is a feeling that you'd think I'd have gotten used to. I haven't.

Before heading out the door, I wish myself "Merde" and "Toi, toi, toi" and "Hals und Bein bruch" (see cast recording) and all that. I'll see you later.

THE LAST ENTRY

MONDAY, SEPTEMBER 10:

It's over. I have never had a weekend so full of Fierce Moments in my life. I had neither time nor energy to sit down after each show to write about what was happening. Nor did I want to, for fear that putting it down would wake me from the incredible dream I was living. Let me start at the beginning.

I got to the theater at 3:30 to run some things before everyone else got there at 4:00. I warmed up, ran my lines for myself, and wasn't too nervous. I worked the moment where I have to drop the blue blanket into the garbage can while kissing Cady. It's a blind drop, behind you, and it's really tough. Matthew has gotten it down to a science. It's the button of the number, so I wanted to nail it. I tried to train my muscle memory to know where the can was. Worked eight times out of ten. The girls, then Warren and Steve, came in. I got my show shoes. (It's important to work in your shoes before you go onstage. My shoes ground me. Putting on a foreign pair before a show is risky. Your balance and movement come from your shoes.) We ran "I Wanna Be a Producer." Right from the get-go I was making stupid mistakes. Mistakes caused by nerves. I had been doing these movements and saying these lines for eight months. Now that I had bodies around me I was getting crazy. It was frustrating. But this was my dress rehearsal, in a way, so I was happy. *Big rule of theater: bad dress rehearsal, good opening.* I almost wish for it to happen. At the very least, I want *something* to go wrong. It keeps me honest. Things progressed nicely once I got out of my own way. The girls were very excited for me. They all wished me well. Angie winked at me knowingly. Angie and I have been in the same place with this understudy thing. Even though they have not named first and second covers, everyone can tell who they are favoring. And that's fine. That's the job. And management does a good job of keeping it fair, giving people time, letting them know what's up. Angie and I both figured that we would be the "second covers," for Ulla and

Leo. And we were okay with that. When Steve told me I was going on as Leo for half a week, Angie was happy for me. One of us was getting the chance that we didn't think we were going to get.

Cady came in and we ran "That Face." I am used to leading my partner, helping her with lifts and such. It's the natural thing to do, but Cady doesn't need that. She is in control of everything and my attempts to help her were actually hindering. So she helped me to relax a bit and not push everything. By the end of the rehearsal, I was looking at the number in a new way. It could be more relaxed than I had been doing it, less rushed, more fluid, and, in the end, more fun. It was a great comfort to have that from her.

After everyone else left, Steve wanted to run the "Gimme My Blue Blanket" hysteria with me to see what I had been working on. He gave me some suggestions, we worked through them, then he left. I was alone onstage, empty house, full brain. I started at the top of the show. I said all my lines full voice, hearing the responses in my head. (If someone was watching in the house, it probably sounded like one side of a strange phone call.) I went through the entire show, songs, scenes, and craziness, even marked out my costume changes. I was ready. There was nothing else I could do. I looked at the time, almost 6:00. I tried the blanket drop into the garbage can a couple more times. Not too bad, four out of five. I called Melissa but her phone wasn't on. I went out to grab some dinner, even though I wasn't hungry. I ended up with a glass of carrot-celery juice and a nutrition bar. I got back to the theater and readied myself for the 6:30 meet with Nathan.

Six-thirty came and went and Steve told me that Nathan hadn't come in. He asked if I wanted to run lines. So we did. Melissa came in, bringing flowers and a kiss, and watched as we ran lines through the show. A whole slew of flowers were delivered from Ann and Gene, Dennis, and Megan Sikora, a friend at *42nd*

Street. My mind was racing now. When I saw Melissa, I felt this rush of nerves. I don't know why. (The idea that I could feel her support and her nerves, too? Did my seeing her remind me of the impending performance? Or was it simply that I love her and was glad to see her? Probably all of the above.) Steve and I ran lines till 7:00, Melissa left, after a huge hug and kiss, and once again I was alone. This time in Matthew's comfy dressing room. I put my Chuck Mangione *Children of Sanchez* CD in and started washing up.

At about 7:15 I went to Nathan's dressing room to check in with Poppa. We decided to go onstage and run a few physical moments. I wanted to do the "catch" in "Keep It Gay" when Nathan faints and Matthew catches him. It went fine. Then I asked if we could quickly go through "Leo and Max" just so I could see spacing. My legs are so friggin' long, I didn't want to step on his foot or anything. So we ran it. Being onstage with Nathan, both of us in lazy clothes, with canes, to an empty house, doing the final number — definitely a Fierce Moment. We discussed a couple of other smaller bits, and that was it. Nathan told me to "just have fun." He smiled and walked off to his dressing room.

I have to admit that my nervousness about Nathan has subsided. I've been working on that intensely. If I had kept on being nervous around him, there was no way I could have stayed with him in a scene or given him anything close to a solid performance. So I have had to take him down from the pedestal I've put him on. I can still respect and admire him, I just don't have to be afraid of or be intimidated by him. That's certainly not what he wants.

I checked in with stage management to tell them that Nathan and I had connected and that everything was cool. I went back to Matthew's dressing room, where Mark Trezza, Matthew's dresser, was ironing my show shirts. He asked me about my preshow rituals. What did I want to drink — tea or coffee or whatever — before the show, what did I want at intermission, when did I want to get dressed? Having a star dresser is pretty cool, I've learned. Mark is great. He's like an Italian mother.

Mark left and I had about fifteen minutes to chill out before half hour. I sat on the couch and tried my best to meditate. But my mind couldn't stay focused for more than a few minutes. I wanted to go through the lines again and again, but remembered *The Untouchables* scene where Andy Garcia is checking his gun. Sean Connery asks him, "Didja check it already?" Andy says, "Yeah." Sean replies, "Well, don't check it again." If it was fine when you last took a look at it, you're only going to screw it up by futzing with it. So I refrained from running myself ragged. It was then that I let it all go. I told myself, the show is going to be whatever it's going to be. I have prepared as best as I know how.

Me as Leo Bloom, relaxing backstage.

There is nothing left to be done. That's when they called half hour. *No turning back.* Mark came in. I got "miked" up and went into Hair for my 'do. Ashley, one of the violinists in the pit, had agreed to take some candid black-and-white shots of me, as I got ready. I wanted to have some remembrances of the situation, so he casually roamed around snapping pictures of me here and there.

Before I knew it, it was "five" and Mark was putting my suit jacket on me. I looked in the mirror, and there stood a very tall Leo Bloom. Everything looked great. My voice felt good, my body felt good, my mind was . . . racing. There was a part of me that was scared, but you learn to love that. You either love it or you do something else. I went upstairs and said my "hello"s to the stagehands stage left (see section on backstage rituals) and walked out onstage to the preshow gathering. They all wished me luck. Peter Marinos was tearing up as I approached him. He said, "You look so handsome." And smiled to push the tears away. If I haven't expressed it enough, Peter is the Broadway romantic among us. He gets emotional at Broadway debuts and at under-studies going on for the first time. It's lovely and it reminds me what's important. Nathan wished me luck and the lights dimmed. The overture began and, for the third time, I was alone. Everyone else was either onstage (Nathan and the ensemble) or working (Mark) or in their dressing rooms because they didn't come on till later (Cady, Gary, Roger, Brad). So I had some more time to myself. I went back downstairs and roamed around a bit. It felt very strange not to be onstage during "Op'ning Night." My sense memory kept setting off alarms when my usual cues came, telling me that I should be onstage with Naomi. I decided to go to stage right and watch. If I could see it happening with-out me, maybe my mind would take it easy. It sort of helped. I sang along with the ensemble to warm up a bit more. But basi-cally I just buzzed around, walking in circles. The stagehands all congratulated me and wished me luck. Everyone was pulling for me, but I was too nervous to take it in. Ira told me what Matthew usually does (makes faces at Bryn while she's dancing), so I tried that. It didn't help. Finally, I just grabbed my briefcase and coat, took one final swig of water from Mark, and got ready to go behind the door. I heard my cue, the Blind Violinist's final solo, that just yesterday was my own, and I took a deep breath.

– ONSTAGE –

No entrance applause. Good. I didn't expect it. I was prepped for that. Just move on. Say the lines.

I said my first lines and looked around. The spotlight was so bright on me that I couldn't see the audience at all.

Good. Can't see the audience. Keep talking. Get to Nathan.

I gave Nathan the cue to erupt from the newspapers, and he scared me to death. Of course, I knew he was there, but my adrenaline was pumping so high I completely lost it for a good three seconds. Nathan came over to me with his, "Who are you? What are you doing here? Speak, dummy, speak!" I felt a wave of energy (I am not kidding here) go right through and around me as he approached and cornered me. Tropical Storm Nathan. It was yet another Fierce Moment. I had never felt anything like it before.

I said, "Scared. Can't talk." Got a laugh.

Omigodomigodomigod. I got a laugh. I got a laugh. Thank you, God.

The rest is a blur. At 11:00 I was at the other end of one of the best performances of my life. Things clicked, bits landed, laughs came. At one point in the first scene Nathan called me "Big Boy." I wanted to laugh but nerves held it together. The audience was tentative about me at first, but I felt that I won them over. If I didn't get a laugh on something, I just moved on. There were only a couple of physical things that I did wrong. I stepped on two of Nathan's laughs, but knew that I could fix that. At the intermission Nathan turned to me and said, "You're doing a great job," and smiled broadly. That was all I needed. Brad O. turned to me and said, "Poppa seems very happy."

Steve came down during intermission and said, "It's going well." He started to give me some notes, but I think my face made him reconsider. He said, "I'm only giving you these because I know you can handle them. You're doing really well." The notes were about deepening some motivations and making the character a bit more dimensional. I appreciated them and applied them to the second act.

In the second act I felt confident and assured. Matthew's second act is a bit tamer than his first. "That Face" is major, but it went well and it's all downhill from there. Nothing compares to the first twenty minutes of the show. By the way, the blanket went in the can. "Till Him" went well. Better than I thought it would. I thought I was going to be tired and my voice wasn't going to be strong. But I had everything. By the time we got to "Leo and Max," I was basking. The curtain call came and I never stopped smiling. For a few moments I stopped judging what I was doing, stopped checking how I was "being." I just let myself enjoy the applause.

After the show, everyone congratulated me and seemed almost as thrilled as I was that I had done it. It had gone without a hitch. Steve said, "That was amazing. Great second act, Jeff." When Warren appeared in the doorway, he had tears in his eyes. I was moved. He said wonderful things, too. I was glad that they were happy. Dennis came in with Michael Riedel. Ann came in with Dani Super (from Pat McCorkle Casting), Jeremy Rich (casting director from Roundabout Theatre), and Jamie Beth Margolis (from Johnson-Liff Casting). They were all very complimentary and grateful for the tickets. It was fabulous.

Melissa came in and said, "Everyone is talking about you outside." I got changed and we headed out. Michael wanted to take us (Dennis, Melissa, myself, and Mylinda Hull — "Anytime Annie" in *42nd Street*) to dinner at Orso. I signed some programs at the stage door. I thanked people for staying to see me. As we crossed Eighth Avenue on our way to Orso, there was a twelve-year-old kid walking in front of me. He turned around, looked at me, and his eyes bugged out. He then said, very adult-like, "What a great show. Nice job. Wow." I asked him his name, introduced myself, and then thanked him. It was nice to see a young man so confident in his love of theater. I wish more kids were that way. He had a great time, and he gave me a lift as well.

We got to Orso, and Michael, who is a regular there, introduced us to the maitre d'. Michael said, "This is Jeffry Denman. He just went on for Matthew Broderick in *The Producers*." The maitre d' replied, "Oh, you're going to have some fans tonight. There are a number of patrons who came in talking about you. Congratulations." As we sat down, there was some waving of hands and a smattering of applause at three of the tables. A woman came over to thank me for the show and told me how much she enjoyed it.

After a while, I went to the men's room. As I descended the stairs, Dennis came bounding after me. "I just had to talk to you," he said. "So what are you going through? What was it like? How do you feel?" I told him, "You want to know what? It felt right. It felt completely right. Like that's where I belonged. I have felt like an understudy in the past, being onstage with big stars.

But this time, I didn't. I don't know if that was me or the situation or what. It just felt right." Dennis picked up his cell phone and called John Erik to report a Fierce Moment.

I woke up Saturday morning to my door buzzing. My brothers and their wives had arrived. Bob and Anne were, unfortunately, unable to bring their two adorables, Molly and Sarah (my goddaughter). We got them settled and began to plan the day. I had a slew of uncles and aunts coming in who I had to connect with. Most of them would see *42nd Street* when they weren't seeing *The Producers*. So we headed down around 11:30 and found them at noon. I headed to the theater at 12:30 and left them with Melissa at the Starstruck diner. Aunt Libby (my godmother and my mom's sister) and Uncle Bert (my mom's brother) were coming to my matinée. I also had more casting folk coming, Alison Franck from Papermill Playhouse and Howie Cherpakov from the Weisslers. Ann had left two bottles of champagne and glasses at the theater for me. We had been without the night before. She brought it over to share with the casting folk and my family.

At 12:30 I got some notes from Warren and Steve. Most of the things I knew about and had noted during the performance. Some of them were just mishaps that might happen to anyone any night of the week. The rest were tweaks in motivation, which I liked. I tried to replicate my preshow process from the night before. I listened to the same music, did the same things in the same order.

Now I was worried about a second-show slump. When you have a big opening night or an exciting first performance as an understudy, a bit of letting-up can happen on the second night. It's natural. But if you know it's coming, you can play against it. That was my goal, to be even more prepared than I had been the night before. Problem was, the nerves had calmed. My brain knew that I had done it and done it well. I had to convince myself that I still needed to be nervous, because that's what would keep me sharp. By the time the overture began, I was nervous again and happy.

The first act went well. I remember thinking during the "Keep It Gay" scene, "Wow, the end of the first act is so far away!" The audience was great. I got bigger laughs. They seemed to accept me a bit sooner than on Friday night, which I was grateful for. I kept thinking of my Aunt Libby watching me. She danced as a young girl, and she always has had a special connection to me because of that. So appropriate that she's my godmother.

During our breaks between scenes, Nathan and I towel off, get water, and change costumes. Friday night there was no talking between us. In the first act of the Saturday matinée, it was pretty much the same. I didn't mind. He seemed to be having fun with me onstage. It wasn't like the fun he has with Matthew, but he didn't seem distant. It's hard to explain.

During the intermission, Steve Z. came into my dressing room and told me, "Mel and Anne are here and want you to stick around after the show so they can talk with you." Excuse me? That would be Mel Brooks and Anne Bancroft, and you're telling me this now? *At the intermission!*

I acted calm, thanked him, and he left. I turned to Mark and pumped my fist Tiger Woods style as he smiled. "Yes! Yes!" I screamed. I got over my nervousness. I realized that I was having a fabulous show and was glad that they got to see me. Steve's words from the previous day went through my head again: "I'm only telling you these things because I know you can handle it." I was handling it.

Act Two went great. The audience just got better and better.

As the second act started, Nathan and I were at the door getting ready to enter.

NATHAN: Having fun?
ME: Yes.
NATHAN: Well, good.

During "That Face" I got the blanket in the can again. A bit of the tip hung over the edge, but the weighted part was in like Flynn. Heh heh.

Steve was the first to come into my dressing room after the show. He reminded me that Mel and Anne were coming down. He wanted to know if I wanted to do notes now or later. "There's only a couple. I'll give 'em to you now." So he gave me more tweaks and left as my Uncle Bert and Aunt Libby came in. They were ecstatic. My Aunt Libby was in tears. Uncle Bert smiled as wide as his ears would let him. I told them both, "You have to stay, because Mel Brooks and Anne Bancroft were at the show and are coming down." Well, my Aunt Libby nearly fell over. And I mean that. I had to grab her and take her to the couch. She told me what a fan of Anne's she was, not to mention Mel's. Bill Germano from Routledge came in. He loved the show. My brothers and their wives (who had come over with Melissa after seeing *42nd Street*) came in along with some friends of mine who had — amazingly — gotten tickets to my show by standing in line for cancellations. I couldn't believe it. Holly Chapman (my masseuse) entered with her massage table. As we were introducing everyone to everyone else, Aunt Libby came rushing over whispering, "They're here, they're here." Mel came bounding in yelling, "Jeffry Denman!" He grabbed my face and kissed me on both cheeks. Anne stood there in all her loveliness, smiling broadly. The things they said to me in those few minutes will forever live in my heart. I'll keep them there. Mel had only one note for me.

MEL: Oh Jeffry, in the excerpts from your manuscript that you gave me, you missed one thing. When I said that I would have to try to be humble at the Tony Awards, it got the biggest laugh of the night. You couldn't hear that. You gotta fix that. Everything else is great.

ANNE: (indicating Mel) From this one? That's your *only* note. Can you believe it?

After they left, I turned to my friends and family and said, "I'm glad you were all here to witness that, because you never would've believed me if I had told you." We opened champagne and toasted and laughed and smiled. Fierce Moments abound.

I got my massage from Holly while my family dined with Melissa at Sam's. I felt great afterward. My brothers and their wives were coming to the evening show, as was my friend Noah Racey. He had sent a bottle of champagne back beforehand. I knew we'd use it.

The evening show was good. The audience wasn't as vocal as at the matinée but that's normal for a Saturday-night crowd. (Saturday-night audiences usually have full stomachs and lots of wine rolling around their brains, so they tend to be a bit quieter than at Saturday matinées. And I can understand. If I had to work nine to five, five days a week, I'd try to pack in as much escape into the weekend as I could.) But Saturday night was the first performance where I felt in control of what I was doing. I could watch myself more. It's the last thing an actor is supposed to do, but in this situation I had to. I had to watch myself — just for a moment — up there opposite Nathan Lane in *The Producers*. I experimented with Leo a bit too. It became great fun. My voice was tiring, though. The first twenty minutes of the show is murder. The rest of the show, you can pace yourself, but that first twenty is tough. Now it was about my endurance. I had put so much into these first three performances, I was worried that I wouldn't have enough for Sunday. That's when my entire family was coming, including Jim Deiotte. I wanted to sound good, especially for Jim.

At the intermission, Steve came into my dressing room. He had two things to say. Number one, he had no notes. Number two, Matthew is taking a personal day next Sunday. He wanted me to do the show. I said okay and thank you. After he left, I sat down. This meant a lot to me. His decision cancelled the domino effect that I thought would keep me from going on in the future. Fierce Moment. Ray Wills came down and told me that Roger Clemens and Sandy Koufax were in the audience. Way cool.

After the show, Noah came back with my brothers. Alison Franck came back and congratulated me. Howie Cherpakov, the other casting director, had to leave right after the show. He ended up sending me a lovely card on Sunday. Melissa brought over my Uncle Pete, Aunt Kay, Uncle Joe, and Aunt Joyce, who had just seen the evening *42nd Street*. After enjoying Noah's champagne, we all made our way upstairs. As we headed down the alley toward the stage door, I noticed Nathan in front of us. As he exited, the crowds called out for him to sign their programs and shake his hand. Uncle Pete said, "Lead the way, Jeffry." I opened the stage door. It took them a second to recognize me, but they did. Two girls asked me to sign their posters. Nathan was doing the same en route to his car. On the other side of the barricade, fans yelled, "Nathan! Nathan!" He went over and signed a few more before getting into his car. That's when I heard "Jeffry! Jeffry!" intermingled with "Nathan! Nathan!"

Way Fierce Moment.

As Melissa and I walked home, we talked about next Sunday. When we had closed *Cats*, underneath all the excitement was the feeling that it was the end, too. There would be no more shows. I had felt the same about this past weekend, that it was my *one time* to do what I could and accept the fact that I probably wouldn't get the chance again. But now there would be more, and that made me very happy. I slept well.

SUNDAY, SEPTEMBER 9:

My dad hates New York, so to see him here does my heart good. I know he's making a sacrifice for me. As soon as I met him at the hotel he said he wanted to pick up the tickets, so we did that, then headed back to the hotel, where I found my mom. We all headed over to Puleo's for lunch. There sat Fred and Jim with all of my uncles and aunts, including Uncle Garry, who had come in with my parents that morning. It was a wonderful sight.

Melissa picked up her mom at the Port Authority and made her way over by 12:30. We sat and had lunch, enjoyed wonderful conversation, took pictures, and laughed. I couldn't have been more excited. By 2:00 we were ready to start the trek. We got Fred situated with Melissa's mom in the theater. The rest of us went back to the Milford to change and clean up. I got a call from Luis Villabon, my friend who was assisting Paula Abdul. I knew what the message was going to be before I got it. Only one reason why he'd be calling. She'd cancelled. Apparently she hadn't known it was a matinée.

I went downstairs to get ready. Blood was pumping and adrenaline was flowing. It had all led up to this. This show was for me. I had nothing to prove, no one to introduce myself to, as I had with the casting directors. These were all people who loved me and knew me. That's why I'd organized it that way. I wanted my last performance to be for love.

The show went great. I enjoyed every minute. Laughs were good. (The blanket went in the can for the fourth time in four tries. Perfect score. Look out, NBA.) More fun than I had had in a long time. For the briefest of moments, I almost felt as though it were really me starring in the show. Nathan seemed to be more comfortable with me now. We talked during the costume changes. Acting with Nathan this weekend taught me more about performing than I had learned in thirty years. I was looking for nothing and he gave me everything. I thank him from the bottom of my heart for four of the most exciting and challenging performances I've ever been involved with. His trust in me, and the audiences' reactions, filled my heart over and over. I will be drawing from that account for a long time.

At the end of the show, during the curtain call, I was finally able to see Melissa in the audience. Cady nudged me and said, "Look at your girl." She was standing with her mom, applauding madly and crying. I got choked up. I tried to see the rest of my folk, but couldn't.

After the show I quickly undressed and threw my robe on. Because Fred couldn't do the stairs, I wanted to bring the celebration to him. I went to get Melissa to help me with the glasses and champagne. When I got to the stairs, I looked up, and my dear friend Nancy Lemenager was staring down at me. In the seven years that I have known Nancy, I have never seen her speechless. She is usually the one who has the right thing to say — very cool, very collected, appropriate, and supportive. She was speechless. All she kept saying was, "Jeff, oh my God, oh my God." I have been on the other side of that reaction many times, and it's wonderful either way. She started to tear up and hugged me tight. I thanked her for coming and for her support. I asked her if she could help me with the glasses. I went upstairs to get Melissa. As I rounded the corner toward the stage door, she was right there. She had been crying. She grabbed me and kissed me and hugged me.

Somehow I felt validated. I know that sounds insecure, but what have we learned? Actors *are* insecure. Melissa and Nancy and Dennis, the staunchest supporters I have, are also the most honest with me. They don't pull punches, they tell the truth. In every case, their tears had told me something. I had succeeded in translating what's inside of me to the stage. This past weekend, I was able to show audiences the contents of my heart. That's what they want to see. That's why they come and pay the money. We must give it to them. I don't care if you're doing *The Full Monty*, *Stomp!*, or the *Radio City Christmas Show*. At the heart of every theatrical performance is that challenge. To change, alter, enhance, deepen, and magnify the hearts of people who sit there watching. I'm a performer. I live for that challenge.

Nancy, Melissa, and I gathered glasses and the bottles of champagne and took them up to the house. As I entered the theater, I saw that almost everyone had exited the orchestra seats, which was good. My family and friends applauded me vigorously, making other audience members look over. I hugged and kissed everyone. My dad was quiet and calm. He just stood there and said, "We are so proud of you. You continue to top everything you've done before. I just love watching you." My mom said, "Honey, you were so wonderful. And to have Fred here and everyone else. You've made it so special."

We made our way to the lobby, opened the champagne, and started pouring. We toasted and I thanked them all for being there. Some remaining audience members came over and congratulated me. A young woman in a wheelchair came over and asked for my autograph. We took pictures everywhere, finished up the champagne, and parted. I took my parents down to my dressing room with Melissa. Everyone else headed to Sardi's. We put the glasses away, and I gathered my things. I showed my dad

that I had used *Children of Sanchez* as inspirational music before
the shows. He had introduced it to me when I was nine. We
headed up to the stage door and made our way out. Fred was outside waiting for a friend to pick him up. Jim was going to wait
with him, then meet us. As I said goodbye, some fans came over
and asked for my autograph. Fred smiled. I thanked him for
coming and said goodbye. My mom kissed him and said goodbye. She worries about him so much. She's a nurse and took care
of him during some cardiac rehab a few years ago. He has been a
true friend and spiritual mentor to both of us for as long as we've
known him.

We made our way to Sardi's. I marveled at my wonderful life.
I thanked God for all of it.

At Sardi's a few cast members had shown up — Kimberly,
Naomi, Christina, Jennifer, and Ray — along with Connie from
Wardrobe and Tommy, one of the stagehands. Ann and Gene
came in soon after. They, along with my family and friends, occu-
pied the upstairs bar and a bit of the dining area. We sat down
and ordered dinner. Before it arrived, Melissa put a blue box in
front of me. I unwrapped it. It was a hatbox. Inside was a beautiful black fedora, exactly like the one that Matthew and Nathan
(and now I) wear in the show at the end. Inside, a piece of white
cloth had been embroidered:

"Bloom's Day — Sept. 9, 2001 Love, Mom, Dad & Melissa"

I started to cry.

MONDAY, SEPTEMBER 10:

Now we're up to date. It's Monday. Monday night to be exact.
The only other thing I did today (other than write my butt off)
was go to the Yankees–Red Sox game, because Roger Clemens

was supposed to pitch. I called Barlow/Hartman (PR) and with the help of Joe Perotta (an old friend from Buffalo theater) tried to figure out if I could meet Clemens after the game. He got me in touch with their PR person and she said she'd make it happen, as long as they won. If they lost, it was off.

Melissa and I went to Yankee Stadium with high hopes. About five minutes before the game was to start, it started to pour, and it rained hard for a good half an hour. Once it let up, they started working on the field, but to no avail. They called the game about 9:00. I told Melissa I was still going to try to meet him. After all, they didn't lose, did they?

After dropping some names that I had been told to drop, we were taken to the Yankee parking lot, where we were to wait for Roger to come out. He eventually arrived and seemed very happy to see me. Someone had told him I was there. We shook hands and congratulated each other. The people who were with him — his wife and friends — had all seen the show. They had enjoyed themselves and were very friendly. I noted how *huge* he is. He asked me what it's like being an understudy. I said it's kind of like being a relief pitcher. Someone else does all the hard work and gets the glory; you just make sure nothing goes wrong when they leave. I thought it was pretty appropriate. I wished him luck in his quest for twenty wins. At this point he's nineteen and one. I think he's gonna do it.

I called my dad as Melissa and I made our way back to the subway. I told him where we were and what had happened. I described the evening as the cherry on top of the whipped cream. (A perfect way to end the weekend.) Melissa laughed at my cliché, but that's what it felt like.

One year. Wow. It would be easy to consider this the end of a great period in my life. But it doesn't feel that way. It feels more like a beginning. I have always tried to welcome whatever life has brought me, knowing that the bad and the good will ebb and flow. The moment I realized that the happier I became.

As we rode the subway home I thought back to a year ago. *Cats* closing. The dreams and hopes I had for the coming year. Did they come true? Not all of them. But others that I hadn't even thought of did. And you won't hear me complaining about any of it.

ACKNOWLEDGMENTS

FIRST AND FOREMOST, I would like to thank Mel Brooks and Susan Stroman. Their talent and genius made this journey worth being written about. My agent, Ann Steele, and her husband, Gene Jones, helped me in ways too numerous to mention. My girlfriend, Melissa Rae Mahon, was always there to listen, help, and put up with countless nights of "I'll be right in, honey. I just have to finish this entry." Steve Jakiel, my first high school English teacher, made me keep a daily journal and threw out a vocabulary test I failed because of a show I was in the night before. Jim Deiotte and Lynne Formato awoke and nurtured the performer in me. Paul Kolnik and Ashley Horne were generous with their time and talent for photography. The cast and crew of *Cats* made the show — especially the closing — a wonderful experience. The entire *Producers* family made this year live up to its hype. Bill Germano was patient and helpful and made my first foray into the world of book writing a pleasure. One I plan on repeating. And finally, I thank my family — who continue to amaze me in their ability to love and support — and especially my parents, Bob and Maggie, who should be awarded a special Tony for Outstanding Performance by an Actor's Parents.